Major Disaster -

Lessons Learned

By: Eve Gonzales

Printed in the United States of America

Second Printing, 2016

ISBN-13: 978-1537636634
ISBN-10: 1537636634

G.L Skye Publishing
Front Royal VA 22630

Book Layout, cover art and design created and Copyright ©
by G.L. Skye Publishing

www.greatlivingsource.com

This book is dedicated to

God who gave me the ability to accomplish all I have done in my life.

To my wonderful husband, son, and daughter who have supported me along the way and endured my times of absence while I was away responding and helping others.

To my parents who pushed me to be more than I ever thought I could be and never gave up on me.

To Bob, my Vice President, long time missionary partner, and dearest friend who has walked the last 17 years of this journey with me; holding true to the vision and helping Caring Hearts to accomplish the many things we have done.

To all the CHI board members past and present and all the volunteers who ever assisted in any of the disaster responses we participated in and to all the people who attended my training classes and encouraged and requested me to write this book.

Thank you from the bottom of my heart for your support, encouragement, assistance, and desire to be prepared

"Freedom is never more than one generation away from extinction. We didn't pass it on to our children in the bloodstream. The only way they can inherit the freedom we have known is if we fight for it, protect it, defend it, and then hand it to them with the well fought lessons of how they in their lifetime must do the same. And if you and I don't do this, then you and I may very well spend our sunset years telling our children and our children's children what it once was like in America when men were free."

-Ronald Reagan 1961

The journey for this book began over 12 years ago when our non-profit entered the world of disaster relief. From the very first tsunami, and then hurricanes, earthquakes, floods, fires, mudslides, typhoons, and nuclear meltdowns, each new event taught me more about human nature, costly errors in judgment, thought processes, and consequences of the failure to be prepared whether by an individual, a county government, or a country. In my exhaustion of seeing loss of life and disaster victims, I sought a way to change the outcome of any type of disaster that could only happen if people, communities, and governments took the threats of disaster seriously and prepared.

My first step was to communicate to individuals and families a program that would help them prepare in just minutes a day. It is called *Preparation Made Simple*. I began touring the United States sharing with people the critical lessons I learned through each event and the important information everyone needs to know so that they don't become a victim.

At the request and encouragement of many of my lecture attendees, I wrote this book. Because the world is changing at such a fast pace and laws just as quickly, some guidelines (in regard to state and federal laws) may be outdated by the time you read this book. Regardless of any changes, the information in this book should open your eyes to what you should expect and help you prepare so that you, your family, and those around you will not become unnecessary victims.

Unfortunately, I am restricted from sharing certain information, especially on medical advice, but I have done my best to give you as much information as I am allowed in order to set your focus in the right direction. Now the rest is up to you.

Don't get overwhelmed in the process of preparation (as many make it harder than it really is). Just be diligent, determined, and steadfast. Please choose to be prepared and then teach others to do the same. There is strength and safety in numbers. The more who prepare and can handle whatever comes their way, the stronger we all will be and the better the outcome for us all.

Chapter 1

Before we look at how you can avoid the same mistakes others have made, we first must look and understand why so many are caught unprepared or simply choose not to prepare.

Disaster Preparedness = Self Reliance

Are You Ready?

Natural and man-made disasters are becoming increasingly common - earthquakes, tornadoes, flooding, hurricanes, fires, and even random acts of violence and terrorist attacks can strike swiftly and with little warning. Every year thousands die and millions worldwide are driven from their homes. If it happens to you, will you know what to do? Will you have enough of the necessary supplies? Do you have a 72-hour emergency kit in your car if you must evacuate immediately? Do you have an emergency escape plan or meet up plan for your family? Do you know alternative medical options for when medical services are not available? Do you have a plan on how to protect those you love? Do you have enough relief supplies in your home to get you through at least 6 months? For most people, the answers to all the above questions are - NO.

As a crisis first responder, I have seen thousands caught totally unprepared. They had no food, no clothes, no shelter, no plans, no money, and no idea of what they should do. The following are some of the excuses we hear all the time as to why people are not prepared:

1. Nothing has ever happened here so why bother.

2. I don't have the money to prepare.

3. I will deal with it when it happens.

4. I don't know where to begin.

5. My spouse does not want to waste money.

6. Why bother when the government and others will give us what we need?

7. I have no place to store it.

8. Random acts of violence and terrorist attacks will never happen where I live.

These are excuses we hear over and over again; these are also the people who have been, and will be, standing in long lines waiting for assistance in a state of shock and waiting for others to instruct them on what they need to do. They will follow anyone who gives them instructions even if the directions or advice is reckless or ill-advised. Case in point: We arrived at a community that was closed off basically from the rest of their surrounding city. They lived in an island area where the only way into their area was via two bridges. One was completely destroyed and the other was questionable. Our rescue teams made it in though it was not deemed safe for anyone to try to leave the area. When we arrived, people were swimming, bathing, washing dishes, and cooking with water from someone's pool. The whole neighborhood came to this family's house because the owner said their water was safe even though the storm surge went right over his pool. When I saw what was going on, we immediately instructed people to get out of the pool, stop using the water, and not touch us as we knew we were going to have an epidemic on our hands – which we did. There was a huge breakout of Impetigo, a highly contagious bacterial skin infection. If people had taken a moment to think and rationalize the fact that the storm surge went over the pool, and not listened to the advice of one person, they could have saved themselves a lot of pain and suffering.

An example of lack of preparedness and an incorrect mindset one cannot afford to possess if they want to live and thrive after a disaster event occurred at another location outside a disaster danger zone. During one disaster, we were headed to a location that we were told looked as if they had been hit by a weapon of mass destruction. Most homes in that area were condemned and most personal items and even some lives had been lost. There were still people trapped in that area and we were going in to provide relief assistance. On our way, we stopped and met with the National Guard to escort us. We met them at a make shift relief center miles away from the danger zone. When we stopped to check with the relief agency, we saw hundreds of people in a line that were waiting all day for someone to show up with food and water. None was delivered yet. (These people stood all day in 100 degree weather when they could have walked 2 or 3 miles to an area that was not in a danger zone and stores were open.) We were asked to distribute some of our supplies even though we were headed into the hardest hit area where the people could not get out for help. We finally agreed to give them some but explained that we could not give them all of our supplies as they were expected in an area that was in dire need. So we opened up the back of the truck and handed out hundreds of items but it was not enough to feed everyone there. People were pushing and shoving their way to the front of the line while others were screaming and crying for us to give them the rest of what was in our truck but we could not give it all to them. It was heart breaking. There were many young children whose parents stood in the sun all day. Most of the people in line could have helped themselves by walking a few miles but chose to just wait for aid to arrive. Our mission was to get our supplies into the areas devastated by the storm. The people we left crying in a parking lot had the ability to get to better ground but instead were waiting for assistance to come to them; they did nothing to help themselves all day long. That was their plan and it didn't work very well.

Chapter 2

Why People Do Not Prepare

The #1 excuse we hear is:

"Nothing has ever happened here so why bother."

It is very difficult for people to prepare for something that they can't imagine will ever happen. But they do; September 11th happened, hurricanes, tornadoes, earthquakes, floods, tsunamis, and mudslides all happened. And now, more frequently, we see mass shootings and terrorist attacks, not just in foreign countries but here in America as well. The fact is most of these will happen again and if you live in a region where it is possible, then you should be prepared.

Should we live in fear and panic of these situations? Of course not. Should we live as though they will never happen to us, absolutely not. Preparing yourself and your family for a possible disaster does not mean you live in fear. For example, most parents, who have a pool, live by the ocean or on a lake, or those that just want their child to have a life-saving skill, enroll their children in swim classes at a young age. Knowing that their child can save themselves if they fall into the water brings comfort and assurance to all involved. Preparing for a disaster is no different; it brings peace of mind knowing that every person in your family has a plan of action to give them the best chance of survival and the tools and supplies they need to get by. Just as swim lessons are not a bother or waste of money, neither is preparing for a disaster. In fact, the items you spend money on can be used even if nothing happens; therefore, nothing is wasted.

Excuse #2

"I don't have the money to prepare."

Preparing for an unknown disaster does not mean you have to spend a lot of money, and the food you purchase can be part of your food budget since you will eat it sometime anyway. Most of the items you will need, you most likely already have. You just don't have it organized to go at a moment's notice.

At the impending arrival of the tsunami that hit Japan, people were given warning and told to leave immediately. Many died because they were trying to grab as many supplies as they could from their house. If their emergency supplies had been in totes, backpacks, or boxes close to an exit, each person could have grabbed one container, headed straight to their car and been on their way without going back for seconds. If you have to run to each person's room, try to grab clothing, shoes and any other items you might think of, you may not get out in time and you will not get everything you need. Organizing and packing the items you will need during a disaster or evacuation will take time, but if you do it as a family, not only will everyone know where the relief supplies are but it will take much less time getting it done.

Excuse #3

"I will deal with it when it happens."

This is not a plan but a cop-out. How do you deal with a situation like "getting water" when there is none available? In our relief manual, a story is shared about a doctor who never believed anything would happen to him or his family so he refused to prepare. Well, something did happen. A hurricane hit forcing him and his family to live on almost nothing for 2 weeks (one gallon of water and some tuna fish). He greatly regretted his decision and wanted his story shared so other families would not have to endure what his family did. Having been in disaster sites before and having lived through a disaster, the time to prepare is before an event because everything is hard to come by after the event.

Excuse #4
"I don't know where to begin."

This thought can be truly overwhelming and we have all been there. For most people, the thought of cleaning out their garage is overwhelming because it usually is the messiest and most cluttered room we have to clean. So we avoid it at all costs and allow it to get worse year after year until finally we must take action. When the day of the big cleaning comes, we stand there looking at the mountain in front of us, clueless as to where we should begin. The best answer to the problem is to not look at it as a whole so you will not become discouraged. Instead, take one section at a time. In doing this we can see progress and become energized and we will eventually get all the sections done. I can assure you that preparing for a disaster is much less painful than cleaning out your garage. When you attack it from the standpoint of doing one section at a time you will see quick progress and be encouraged to get it all done. The biggest hurdle you have is to decide to prepare; once you do that, the rest is easy.

Excuse #5

"My spouse does not want to waste money."

This reason for some people not preparing is more challenging and CAN cause some to do nothing, but we want to encourage you to take a stand on this issue. Many times we are told one spouse wants to prepare for a disaster and the other does not. One wants to get everything the family might need and the other doesn't want to "waste" their money; so compromise. First, find out why your spouse really does not want to prepare. It might truly be that they just do not know where to begin or it might be that they do not want to be bothered with it and money was never the issue, just the excuse. If your spouse does not want to be bothered with it, tell them you will do it. If they just do not know where to start, tell them you do and that you will do it together. If money is the real reason, tell them that there are many things you can do to be prepared that won't cost anything. If your spouse personally does not want to do anything to prepare and they do not want you spending any money, there are ways you can prepare for your family and get your children involved to give them skills they will need. Remember, you have many items around your house already that could be packed and set aside in the event of an emergency. You can also find many good inexpensive items at rummage sales; everything does not have to be brand new, just in good working condition!

Excuse #6

To all of us, this one is mind boggling and a terrible game plan; it is: **"The government and others will provide all I need."**

Time and time again we have seen this to be what many people chose for their plan. Trust us when we say, it will cause great pain and hardship in your life and your family's life if this is your choice for your relief plan. People think that FEMA's job is to provide them with everything they need after a storm or other disaster strikes. **This is not true**. It is also not the government's or the non-profits' job. We are here to assist and help, but no agency will be able to provide everything you need. You will have to wait with everyone else to get whatever supplies may be available.

One evening, when we were responding after a hurricane, we came to a feeding site that had a very long line of people waiting to get a hot meal. The feeding site was out of water and not a single person in line had any toilet paper to use all day. They were thirsty, exhausted, and distressed over the fact that they had to wait in 100 degree weather for food, and they were really upset that they had to use leaves, newspapers, and magazines for toilet paper. We were greeted with hugs and kisses from other relief workers and all those waiting in line. Praise God we were able to provide the water to this site and also had enough toilet paper to give one roll to each family in line. If we didn't have supplies, who knows how long it would have been before some would have come. So please, do not make this your plan of action. Use it as a supplement if necessary but do not expect it to be quick or complete.

Excuse #7

"I have no place to store it."

Please, let's be honest for just one moment. To say you have no place to store relief supplies is simply just an excuse. You do have a place to store supplies; it might mean you have to clean a small corner in the garage, or a closet, or even under your bed. But you do have a place. You just have to make it!

Excuse #8

"Random acts of violence and terrorist attacks will never happen where I live."

This statement could not be farther from the truth; not in this day and age since random acts can happen anywhere. Here is the problem – it is just so hard to believe it *could* happen that we convince ourselves that it *won't*. We also disconnect from the reality of the situation when we hear about such atrocities happening in the news.

Do you remember the first time you heard about someone being decapitated? Do you remember the shock and repulsion you felt over the thought that one human being would do that to another? What about today when you hear those same reports on the news, do you feel the same way? Most likely you do not because you are now used to hearing about it and comfort yourself with the false knowledge that it will never happen to you or anyone you know because things like that do not happen in your town or even your state. Unfortunately, the reality is that people have begun doing unspeakable things we never would have dreamed possible where we live. Unhinged, vengeful, heartless individuals and groups are walking into family restaurants, schools, nightclubs, grocery stores, etc., with a mindset to kill; and they **DO** kill. Sometimes they have a specific target, and for others, it is anyone they happen to see. Today, we also have teens that walk up to someone and punch them to knock them out just for fun because they made it a game.

If you really think you live where no such acts of violence or terrorist attacks will occur, please take a moment and remember all the bombings and shootings you have heard about over the past several years, their increased frequency, and the fact that I am sure those who were caught in the crossfire never expected it to happen either. If they did, they probably would not have been where they were when the bullets started flying or the bombs went off.

So if you really think you are safe from the violence of this world, please think again as none of us are – BUT – we can learn techniques and skills to help protect ourselves. The first skill you need to become proficient in is observation. Most people are not observant. They go through their day never really paying attention to the people next to them or their surroundings. They are simply trying to accomplish all they need to take care of and block everything else out of their mind, but this habit can be deadly.

When I am training a new recruit, I start by pointing this very fact out to them through examples. Let's see how you would do. I had one new team member and one seasoned member who were flying with me to an event we were participating in. Once we loaded the plane and the new recruit was comfortably sitting in her seat, I told both volunteers to close their eyes. I asked the new volunteer to tell me how many rows to the closest exit door. How many rows to the front, back, and over the wing exits? Then I asked how many compartments to each exit. She opened her eyes and said, "Are you kidding me, how should I know?" Then with her eyes still closed the veteran volunteer rattled off all the correct answers and opened her eyes. I told the new volunteer to get up, exit the plane and re-enter, but this time touch each seat and make a mental note and count as she made her way back to her seat. She did not go willingly but finally did as instructed. After she gave me the correct answers, I explained why. The exercise she just went through was a skill that could potentially save her life. If the plane crashed, she would have fed her mind, prior to the event, exactly where all the doors were so if the cabin filled with smoke, and she had to blindly find her way to an exit, she would know the distance she had to travel by counting seats, or if the plane flipped, by counting out overhead compartments.

The first thing we do when we (my family or team members) walk into a building is to find and point out the exits. Most people only notice the doors they walk through and so when an emergency happens, they all head to the same exit instead of one that may be closer and less crowded. Taking the time to feed your brain this information will help in a crisis because your brain will go into automatic pilot and give you options on how best to respond and the action you should take.

Observation is an important essential skill that can make the difference between being a victim or being a survivor. Since it is not something most practice in their everyday life, it is one you need to train yourself and your family to do. When you are walking down the street or in the grocery store, walk past a person and then ask yourself, what color were their shoes, was there anything that seemed abnormal about their behavior, what color was their hair, etc.?

I did this drill with my daughter every time we went out into public or walked the beach. She never knew what question I was going to ask her so she knew she had to pay close attention to her surroundings. One day, my daughter and I went for a walk on the beach. It was a hot morning and we were the only ones on the beach that we could see. Suddenly, a man in a trench coat came out from the side entryway and headed towards us. My daughter started to say – Mom! – when I immediately pulled out my phone and started taking pictures of him. I acknowledged him by saying "Wow, I can't believe you are wearing that heavy coat on such a hot day. I sent your picture to my husband and all my friends as proof that you were really here." The man was stunned, to say the least. As he passed by us, I turned around and continued to take photos. He was looking at me over his shoulder and again I said to him, "My friends will never believe it." This action was a deterrent for him possibly attacking us when our backs were turned to him. I waited to turn back around until he was well past us, and then we exited the beach and hurried back to our car. Not only did we quickly observe how out of place he was, but we promptly informed him we had sent his picture to many people making him less of a threat.

My daughter caught that the man in the trench coat was out of place and wanted to alert me to that fact. Sometimes, it is their mannerisms, their shoes, bulging objects on their hips, etc. that may call you to question their motives.

During disasters, people will feed on your kindness and the belief you are not observant so they will be able to take advantage or to steal from you. It is your responsibility to be prepared so you can ward it off before you have a serious situation on your hands. This skill also helps you in the event you are a witness to a crime as you will be able to give a better description of the criminal.

Chapter 3
What If It Had Been You?

When you hear of any storm event that caused destruction and death, it makes many of us saddened for those affected, but it also should make you stop and think, "What if it had been me and my family in that storm or devastating event? What would we have done"? When you see the wreckage a tornado creates, it is a wonder that anyone survives. Several of us at CHI grew up in states where tornadoes were a common occurrence and all of our families had a storm plan. Everyone in our families knew where to go for safety in the event we were home alone when the sirens went off. There were always relief supplies in case we were stuck in our shelter after the storm passed since we did not know how long it would be before someone would find us to get us out. As children, our parents went through the drills of what to do and where to go if a bad storm was coming. We knew what to do if we were separated and where our meeting place would be. We went through the drills for house fires and break-ins. Our parents made sure we were prepared. Now we find ourselves all volunteering for an organization that is doing the same thing – trying to help people get prepared to survive and responding to the call for help after the storm hits.

Part of being prepared is having a plan on where to go to survive. If you live in a mobile home, please make sure you have a plan (some other structure) for safety before a tornado or hurricane hits. If you live in a house, everyone needs to know which room they need to take shelter in. If you have a basement, it is a little easier, but if you do not, you need an inner room such as a bathroom or closet. In our house, it is the guest bathroom. When my children were small, I began having drills with them just like my parents did with me. Each child knew where to go. They had their own flashlight (this gives a child a great sense of security) and since they had done it time and time again, they were not panicked when we had to do it for real. They were taught what to do when they were alone and who to contact in an emergency.

We also ran drills in our car because where we lived tornadoes happened all the time in spring and summer, and they didn't wait for us to be at home. There were three times in my children's lives that tornadoes did hit while we were driving and we had to get out of the car for safety. This can be and is a very scary situation. Since we had practiced it so many times, it was like second nature to them. One of the hardest things to do when you are looking at a twister heading straight for you is to remain calm because it is a terrifying sight. If you panic, you can't think straight and that can cause you to make some bad decisions. When you are facing a twister or other emergency, every minute and every choice you make matters and can determine life or death. When you have practiced how to respond, react, or do something over and over again, it becomes second nature during an emergency. Instead of fear, you have a working solution and you act.

The word panic is defined as, "thrown into a state of intense fear or desperation" and can cause people to freeze when they need to be moving. It has been proven that people died because they were frozen in fear. Having a plan usually keeps this from happening because your mind already has the solution.

Chapter 4

Lessons Learned From 18 Major Disaster Zones –
The Importance of Being Prepared!

The first important lesson you must know is that there is a really good chance that NO one is coming to your aid! The second is – You are NOT as prepared as you think you are! In fact, most people who think they are prepared are far from having and knowing what they would really need if a major disaster hit.

When I began writing this book, the first important lesson was that "You are not as prepared as you think you are, but in the past year after responding to another major disaster that affected many counties, I changed the #1 lesson to – "There is a really good chance no one will be coming to your aid!"

Over the years, we have seen a great decline in people donating and volunteering to help people in crisis. In fact, during our latest response effort, people were saying that they would not help because it was the government's job to take care of those affected. Their attitude was – "I am not going to give to help those people. Let someone else do it!" (Many people told us those exact words).

Few funds came in for that relief effort, few volunteers were seen in the disaster zone, county agencies were not equipped with supplies or manpower, and they didn't have an effective response plan. The government was found to be lacking. Thus, weeks after a disaster devastated a vast area; many had not received any assistance. Unfortunately, the goodwill and compassion we so frequently saw 12 years ago during crisis events has greatly dwindled over time and made it apparent that the first thing you need to understand is that the odds of someone coming to your aid is slim to none. As for my original #1 lesson that you are not as prepared as you think you are – Please know, you may have packed kits, taken some training classes, and built up your self-esteem to think you can handle anything that comes your way but the truth is that there is always something more to learn or acquire. In my 18 disaster responses, I did not find anyone who was prepared. In fact, most people were not even close to being prepared which resulted in their standing in long lines and being a "victim."

There is a new group of people that are popping up around the U.S. who my team and I met while lecturing on the importance of preparedness and think you should know about. When we asked these people if they were prepared, they responded with an attitude – "You bet we are!" (I always know when I meet someone like that, I will be able to find some gaping holes in their game plan.) When they allow us to investigate their plans, they are left with the realization they were not as prepared as they thought they were. Most people with this type of attitude actually have established some very dangerous or hazardous plans and protocols.

I would like to share three examples of what we have been told by some people and yet my examples could be many from what we have learned from this type of group. I believe it will give you a clear picture and another reason why you need to be properly prepared and informed.

Example 1 – A man approached me when I was speaking at an event in Kansas. He informed me that he and his team were well prepared. I asked if I could look for a hole in his plan. He smugly replied that I could try but I would not find one. I proceeded to ask him, "What will you do if someone in your team is bitten by a potentially rabid animal?" His response – "Oh, that is simple, we will give that person every antibiotic we have and if in 3 days they are not better, we will cut off the limb where they were bitten." I was stunned. This man was so confidant his plan would work but the truth is his plan is a terrible, misguided, hazardous, game plan. Please note – antibiotics will not heal rabies. Rabies is a virus and antibiotics do not work against viruses. Waiting 3 days and cutting off a limb will also not heal rabies but will create other serious issues for that poor unfortunate victim of ignorance! In my initial disbelieve that anyone could even suggest such a plan, I looked at him and said, "You cannot just start lopping off limbs!" He responded that I should not worry because they had that covered as well – they had a saw! The ignorance astounded me and I explained every flaw in their plan. I even asked what they would do if someone was bitten in the neck by a bat, would they just cut off their head? That got him thinking but he left telling me he believed their plan was still a good one.

Example 2 – At another event in Virginia, we had a team of three hunters come to our booth and they too were way beyond confident in their established plan which was – they had the largest guns and the biggest bullets and they would just take from people what they needed. So I asked them the same question about one of them getting rabies. They just looked at each other with dumbfounded looks on their faces. So I said to the biggest man, "OK, let's look at it this way. You were the one bitten by the rabid animal and your buddies will use their big guns to take you out. They laughed and said, "Exactly!" I told them they needed to stop having a thug mentality, take personal responsibility, prepare their supplies, and get some skills so if someone gets sick they could help each other.

Example 3 – A growing more problematic group of people are those who told us that they will not prepare because they state it is the government's job to give them everything they need. They also boldly said that if the government does not provide it to them, then everyone else must. They told us it is their right to be provided for. They refuse to do anything to help themselves. In disaster areas, this type of person is usually the one pushing their way to the front of the line and quickly turn to a bully mentality when it serves their purpose. They start out pleading, then demanding, and then taking by force. I mention them just so you realize their numbers are growing and you most likely will encounter some of them yourself in a disaster area.

There are many ways to become a victim but lack of preparedness, lack of skills, ignorance, over confidence, and outright laziness should not become your downfall! The person who is truly working to become prepared realizes there is always something more they can learn, more supplies they can gather, and will work silently and diligently to obtain them.

This book is to help you evaluate what you have so you will know where you still need to improve in order to have the best all-around relief plan as possible. We will do it one question at a time!

QUESTION 1
Does your family have and know your game plan, evacuation plan, and where and how you will meet up if you are separated?

Before you can really embark on preparing your disaster relief kits, you first need to form your game plan. This plan is what will make the difference on how you come through any crisis.

Every year at the beginning of tornado or hurricane season, people in the preparedness world always promote to the general public to have an evacuation or emergency plan, but they never really give details on what that plan should be or how to go about forming one, which in turn, keeps many from ever making one.

Unfortunately, most people's game plans are put on the back burner. Some will prepare kits but they have no strategy for if they have to evacuate. They also have no idea where they will meet up with loved ones if they should get separated, and no emergency response procedure. Their plan quickly becomes – "I will deal with it when the time comes." This is even true for disasters that do not require evacuation but do require movement on the part of those in the soon to be affected area such as a tornado, fire, mudslide, etc.

Repeatedly, in all our response efforts, we met the people who made "I'll deal with it when the time comes" their proposed response and saw first-hand the hardship and sorrow that choice – handling it when it happens – created.

Being in stand still traffic with millions of others trying to evacuate; tying family members to trees as a last resort; hiding in a closet as a hurricane storm surge approaches; camping out in your car alongside the road because you have no idea where to go or because you ran out of gas; being separated from your family for weeks with no word on how they are doing; having no water or food for the long trip ahead. These are just a few examples of what we have seen because people thought they would be able to come up with a plan after the crisis began but as they quickly learned – it was too late.

My team and I were responding to a major disaster event and were the first ones into an area that was destroyed by a storm. We were going house to house (actually what was left of each house) to see if there was anyone who remained and needed assistance. Lives were lost in the area we were working but we were searching for those still alive. An 80 year old, feeble, traumatized man came out of what was left of his porch and grabbed onto me and began to cry and shake uncontrollably. For 30 minutes I held this man in my arms while he cried and when I finally got him to calm down, I learned he rode the storm out in a closet and lost the one love he still had in his life – his dog. His house was going to be condemned and he had nowhere to go, or money for his heart medication. I asked him why he did not evacuate and he said he did not know where to go or what to do before the storm reached his area so he decided to just hide in his closet and protect his dog.

During that same event, we found a dad, mom, and three children who remained behind in the storm as well. Their home was also being condemned because it was no longer safe to live in. This family rode out the storm hiding in their closet. Their roof was completely gone, two walls collapsed, and all the windows were blown out. They did not evacuate because the dad assured his wife that the media was just hyping the dangers of the storm, and that they did not have to worry because he was "certain it would go somewhere else". Instead, they took a direct hit. To make matters worse, he did not allow his wife to buy relief supplies; therefore, their 4-month old baby had no formula or diapers. His other children were wet, dirty, and traumatized, and no one had eaten in over 24 hours.

One of the saddest examples of what can happen when you do not have a game plan occurred when we were responding to a different catastrophic event. One family (this also included an aunt, uncle, and cousins) gathered together to ride out what they thought would be a mild event. Things turn from mild to nightmare in an instant for this family. At the last moment, dad and uncle, when they knew they were going to perish, tried to put together a game plan to save some of their lives. Here is the tragic outcome of what happened when a last minute strategy had to be formed: It turned out that I just happened to be the first one into that area after the event when a solitary child walked up to me trembling and dazed. She stared at me for a few moments and then whispered "I lost everyone." I looked at this child and thought she meant she had been separated from everyone but the truth was she was the lone survivor and I was the first one she saw after surviving the storm. That precious little girl not only had survived the terror of riding out a storm, hearing her family members crying and praying before they perished, but she also had to cope with the loss of everyone she loved. It was a very emotional situation to say the least. However, we were able to help that child with the assistance of others who knew and loved her family. If ever there was and is a reason to prepare before a storm, it is so that no one will ever have to endure what that sweet little girl did.

Please understand that making a game plan is a serious responsibility. That is why we are providing steps on how to make your plan so you do not have to be a victim like so many others we have met and worked with.

Sitting down with your family and discussing your determined response and protocol for evacuation, how to meet up if separated, what you will do, etc. provides a number of things:

1. It gives the whole family a detailed path to follow.
2. It diminishes fear of the unknown.
3. It removes panic of not knowing what you will do if something happens.
4. It promotes peace.
5. It builds confidence.

The following are some simple steps to get you started:

Step 1 – Think of the different disasters that are common to your area and the response needed for that event. If it is a hurricane requiring evacuation, then develop a plan in the event you must evacuate to the north, south, east, or west of your area. Find routes that will take you out of heavy traffic and determine at what point you will leave and have a designated place you will go to.

If you are prone to tornadoes, fires, or floods – you and/or your spouse should decide where your safety points will be and do the "what if's" – if this happens, this is what we will do. Once you have planned for the more common events, start thinking about those events you hope never to experience in your lifetime but are real possibilities in our current world atmosphere: terrorist attacks, social chaos, epidemics, etc. Your response to these situations will be very much like the previous but these events will disrupt your life "as you know it" for many, many years.

The goal of this book is to help you address each part of your plan, to help you be prepared and NOT to be a victim. It will take thought, investment into your life and future, dedication, and work, but you can and need to do it.

It may seem a little overwhelming to develop this evacuation plan and it may require you to find or buy a place with others so that you have one, but if you truly want to be prepared it is a step you must do. If you plan to ride out any event at your home regardless of the situation, I would consider finding others of like mind to join with you as there is certain to be civil unrest and there is safety in numbers. Understand, staying put can be a tough choice. We will discuss those hardships in another chapter.

Step 2 – Write down: A) detailed outline for the different types of situations in regard to your meet up points (in the event both adults are at work and the children are with a babysitter, at home alone, or at school and you must or desire to evacuate); B) determine how long you will wait at each location before moving on; C) specify your final destination point. Understand that Step 1 and 2 are vital and require your sincere dedication and commitment. Do not put it off or you will never get it done. Try to accomplish at least a first draft of your plan within one week so you can start sharing it with your family. (Your plan may shift and alter as you really start getting into it but you need to start somewhere. Be open to changes as needed.) Giving yourself a deadline forces you to get it done. Procrastination can be deadly. When you have completed Step 2, continue to Step 3.

Step 3 – Plan a fun family dinner. This will help remove stress that this conversation might create for your children. At dinner talk to them about the importance of being prepared and explain they will be taking an active role in all preparation plans. (No child that can walk is too young to help with preparation or too young to learn what to do during an emergency. Even a toddler can be taught where to go in the event of an emergency.)

It is important that you begin to talk to your children about your family plans so they understand they have nothing to be afraid of. Assure them that this is just in case a storm or other situation happens just as you do when you go to a store and you tell them where to go in the event they get separated from you. You let them know that you are helping them to be prepared so they do not have to be worried about what they will do if something occurs. Explain you are going to help them acquire skills and information that will make them stronger and safer, and that you are going to do it as a family and help each other learn.

Children love to feel they are a part of something and enjoy knowing you care enough about them to keep them safe. They will look at it more as an adventure rather than something to fear. Your attitude will be what is most important. If they sense you are afraid, they will be afraid; if you are over confident, they will become over confident; if they feel you are excited to do this as a family, they too will become excited. So please pick the correct attitude for your children and yourself because it will make a world of difference for the outcome of your preparedness!

Step 4 – At dinner, give each child who would not usually be with you throughout the day a card with the contact information of a family member or friend who lives out of your area who they will contact if they get separated from you during a disaster. They should have this card with them all the time. Those that are old enough should memorize the information but they should also carry it with them each day in their wallet, purse, or backpack since people under stress sometimes forget information. Make sure to explain to your children that you may not have a way to contact them at first because the phones may not be working, which is normal, but explain they need to try to contact the person as soon as they can. If phone lines become available, you will have a check-in person who will be able to give you updates on each other. However, you must also plan for the possibility that the phones may not come back online; this is when meet up points and detailed plans become so important.

Step 5 – Go over the protocol you developed, and then ask them to repeat it to you. You can also write or type the information and give it to each child so they have it to review on their own. Encourage the older ones to help the younger ones learn the family game plan. If your children have a babysitter, you will also need to involve your babysitter and the steps they should take.

A day care provider asked that I teach her and her family what they need to do to be prepared. After the training she devised a game plan of what she would do if a crisis event happened. She determined where she would evacuate with the children if needed, and then gave it to each parent along with a list of emergency supplies they needed to provide to her for their children which she stores at her house. She realized that the children in her care would potentially be her responsibility to protect and provide for (long term) if a disaster occurred. Because she loved the children she baby sat for and understood the ramifications of not being prepared she immediately organized her response plan!

Step 6 – Go over the meet up area in the event you are separated. The older your children, the more advanced a meet up you can have. Teach them where the meet up is and how to get to it. Set up times where you can actually take them to their meet up point/s so they are familiar with them.

When I was in school, a friend's house caught on fire. They frequently practiced fire drills and had a plan of action – each person went out their bedroom window and met up at a tree at the end of the yard. When a fire actually did happen, each person followed the plan, everyone got out alive, and when the firemen arrived all were accounted for. In major disasters a meet up place is imperative or it could be a long time before you know how or where you're loved ones are.

Step 7 – Ask your children if they have any questions. If they ask you if you are afraid something bad is going to happen, tell them "no." Explain that you simply want to make sure they know what to do "just in case" so they will not have to worry.

Step 8 – Make plans to practice safety drills and to run through your strategy scenarios. The more you practice these exercises, the more confident and prepared each family member will become. Each time you practice, make it a family fun time that will be enjoyable for all involved. In doing so, they will want to do it and it will continue to remove any associated fear or stress. These designated practice times are also great for introducing and working on survival skills.

Remember, when something happens – if you have a plan in place, each person will automatically put it into action and begin doing what you prepared for. This will give each one of you a better chance of coming through the event better off than those who will "just figure it out when the time comes."

One fear many people have is "What if they are alone when disaster strikes – will they really survive?" This is an important fear to address and have a game plan for. When disaster strikes, everyone hopes and prays that they will be in a safe place with those they love. They will not have to worry about what has happened to their loved ones and they will be able to handle the situation better because they won't be alone to figure out what to do – or so they think!

Many times disaster or crisis does not afford us the luxury of happening at the perfect moment – when we are gathered with our loved ones. This is why preparing game plans are so very important.

Do you remember where you were when 911 happened? I do. I was approximately 50 miles from home in a hospital (doing visitation as a chaplain). When the event happened, both nurses and doctors who knew me told me what had taken place and told me I needed to get home. My husband was active duty and my 2 children were home alone. At the time we lived on a military base so by the time I got home the base was secured. No one was getting on and no one was getting off! That meant my husband was in one location, my children in another, and I was stranded sitting in a car outside the base waiting to get back in. I was informed by the military guard that it could be at least a day or more before anyone was allowed in. Praise God – we had a family plan and we put it into action. Though we could not communicate with my husband, I was able to activate the plan with my children; and my husband without communication with us also followed the pre-determined plan we devised years earlier.

We were fortunate, we did not have destruction or loss of life, and everyone in our family came through the event just fine, BUT WHAT IF – we never established a plan for my children and were unable to communicate with them? Imagine the panic they would have had if their dad or I had not returned for a day.

Being alone when disaster strikes can be a very scary situation but it can be made easier if you take the time now to establish your game plan. Make clear, easy directions that each individual in your family will follow and do in the event something happens and you are apart from one another. Work on needed skills to build up each other's confidence so when you are called into action, whether by yourself or as a group, each person will know how, when, and where they must act.

My son and daughter did an excellent job in that situation, and have over the years in other situations such as tornadoes and hurricanes. Their stress and ours is greatly reduced because we know that if disaster strikes, we will all go into action until we are able to reunite. We have a backup plan for communicating if phone lines are down, we have a meet up place if we are separated, and we know how long to stay put before we leave. We know skills such as land navigation, personal defense, medical care, etc. and we have also discussed what happens if one of us never shows up.

Over the years, I have been in many "Alone" situations when tornadoes and storms came out of nowhere and action had to be taken. Whether I found myself in a car as a twister touched down or in a home with no basement, I automatically followed my set plan and came through just fine.

Being alone can be a very overwhelming thought, but if you take the time to plan now, it doesn't have to be!

When my children were put to the test on 9-11, they came through perfectly; when twisters were touching down around us while we were driving in a car, they came through with flying colors; when we had to evacuate or when we had to take shelter, whether alone or together, they came through beautifully because they learned what to do and had a course of action to take.

So, whether you are alone or with others, for the most part, the plan is the same. You just have to have one and then follow it.

If you have children in school, we also highly recommend that you find out what your school's protocol is in the event of a crisis or disaster. Some schools will not allow you to pick up your child and will not allow your child to just leave. Knowing what their guidelines are will help you to plan accordingly. If your school does not have a plan, we encourage you to get involved and assist them in making one that will be in your child's best interest, not the schools. Many school districts have passed a response protocol that if a disaster occurs while your child is in school, the school district has authority over your child. In fact, the school can send them where they deem necessary and not inform you of their location until it is convenient for them to do so. You will not be able to pick them up at the school. You will have to wait until the school says it is safe for you to pick up your children. If this is your school's protocol, I suggest trying to get it changed. Regardless, make sure to address it in your family game plan, including the course of action you will take and how the children are to handle it.

I wrote on the topic of the importance of having a game plan several times over the past 14 years and I will continue to do so. I met thousands of people over the years in disaster areas who did not have a plan, relief supplies, separated from those they loved, and had no idea where they were or how to get in touch with them. Each time, it was terrible to see the added distress, worry, and hardship they had to go through. Please – learn from their mistakes and start making your plan today!

Chapter 5

Question 2

Do you have kits that have good working equipment and tools, and are your kits complete?

Most people fail at this. Many people we met in a disaster area did not have complete kits. They had partial, haphazard, thrown-together items that were not well thought through or they went online and purchased individual items or pre-assembled bags and put them aside for an emergency. When it came time to use them, they either did not know how to use the items purchased, or they were so cheap the items broke.

I want to share a true story about a dear friend of mine named Connie (she gave me permission to use her name). I met this woman when she purchased our Survivalist Natural Remedies Kit online. She contacted me so I could help educate her more about the kit and how to use it. Over the months, I began to learn about all the "stuff" Connie had bought in her attempt to make sure her family was prepared. She wasn't sure what she needed and, therefore, bought many inferior products that could and would leave her without useful supplies if an event actually happened. As I started to teach Connie, she began to learn the truth about certain products and the importance of trying them out and organizing them into kits. She then wanted all her friends to learn so they did not make the same mistakes she made. So she organized an all-day training class for me to teach. She set up a second one so they could learn even more. The last training we just completed was a hands-on class so family and friends could acquire essential skills and try out some of the items they purchased. Connie was, and still is, determined to make sure that those around her are prepared as best as they can be! Though she began her preparedness journey attempting to buy and do the best she could to prepare her family, she never tried to use anything she bought and did not realize she was taken advantage of by some sellers she purchased from. However, with her dedication and determination, she learned the importance of research, asking questions, and trying everything out so that she knows it works. She now helps others to do the same.

Having complete kits with good quality tools is vital and will determine how well you will weather the storm. So just as I did with Connie, let us take it one step at a time. We will begin with looking at the kits you will need:

MEDICAL KIT

FOOD

HYGIENE

BABY SUPPLIES

DOCUMENTS

ESSENTIALS

I wrote *Preparation Made Simple* to help people get prepared in just minutes a day. It discusses each kit and what you need in each one of them so I will not be covering that in this book. What I will share is the importance of making sure that each item you put into your kit works! Just because someone is selling something does not mean it will work for you. A good example is that many people buy flint strikers and put them in their kits but many people in disaster areas we helped did not know how to use them and could not get a fire started.

A big error people make is that they do not want to open items they purchased for their relief bag so as not to wear them out, but you need to practice with them! You need to practice setting up your tents, working with your water filters, making fire, etc. If you do not know how to make something work or it breaks the first time you try it, you will find yourself waiting in lines with hundreds or thousands of others.

This is a mental picture for you: Have you ever gone shopping on "Black Friday" where so many people are pushing, shoving, screaming, fighting, and grabbing items they don't really need but that they just want? If people are willing to behave that way for items that are not life sustaining, imagine what it will be like if there is a major crisis and food, water, and other life supporting necessities are in short supply.

We have seen the crying, pushing, fighting, etc. in disaster areas and it is heartbreaking and in some cases terrifying to see. We have also seen people pull together to help each other at the onset of a disaster event which is wonderful and inspiring, but as some told us later, that kindness turned into each man for himself when months began to pass and supplies were difficult, and in some cases impossible to come by.

It is important to have everything you and your family will need so you will not have to rely on others, but also try to have some excess to help others with. These items can also be used to barter with. If you have excess and want to help your neighbors or friends, make sure not to give away what you need – or like others, you will be waiting in long lines for assistance that may never be coming. Some people think that last statement is heartless, but remember this – each person has the responsibility to prepare for themselves. If they choose not to do anything now, that **IS** their game plan for survival and it is not your responsibility to provide them with all that you worked so hard to set aside. It is their choice to be without, not yours. Yes, you want to lend a helping hand if possible but remember your family comes first because your choice was to be prepared!

In disaster relief, we have an important saying – "One is none" because if you only have one of something and it breaks you have none!

Frequently, we are asked by people to evaluate different emergency preparedness pre-assembled bags that are out on the market. Our first advice is – always prepare your own bags and do NOT buy one that is already in a backpack because one bag does not fit all sizes. We are disliked by many people who are trying to make money because of this statement, but hear us out before you shoot it down. If you are buying an emergency relief bag, it is because you think you may have to evacuate, and it might have to be on foot. A bag that fits a 6-foot male will not fit as comfortably on a 5-foot female and vice versa. Buying a bag with no support for the back will cause pain if you have to travel a great distance, which will slow you down.

When you are preparing for a disaster, it is very important to take the time to try on different backpacks for each member of the family and buy ones that fit each person's build, including your child. Once you have backpacks, you can begin filling them with the items you need but make sure not to overload them! Your bag should NEVER exceed 1/3 of your body weight. Remember, the lighter the bag the faster you can move.

Yes, you can buy a pre-assembled, one size fits all bag with cheap nylon rope, glow sticks that don't last, extremely limited medical kit, hygiene, etc. or you can take the time, research and buy items like 550 paracord instead of nylon rope, a good filtration bottle instead of purification tablets, add hygiene items you normally use, acquire a wider range medical kit, and other good quality items you tested and know they work until you have in YOUR bags what YOUR family needs!

I recently read a description of a bag that said it was assembled using the advice of others, which possibly implies they have never been in a disaster where they had to evacuate or try to survive. If they had been, many of the items in their bag would not be there because the quality was poor.

One question you need to ask yourself is – if you purchase a pre-made survival or disaster preparedness bag, can your family and you really survive on what is in it? Really take the time to evaluate it. Will 50 feet of nylon rope help you for all the different ways you might need to use it in a disaster and will it hold up? Our military and our entire disaster relief team uses 550 paracord for a reason. It may cost more but it is worth so much more! Would you be comfortable sleeping in a little tent that gets strung over a rope where both ends are open or would you prefer to buy a two-man tent that zips completely shut and fits into your backpack? Would you rather have peanut butter or some good freeze dried food in your bag? Will you be happy eating the high calorie bars or hockey puck food rations that are in the basic pre-assembled bag? Take each item in the assembled bag and ask yourself if it is what you want for your family? Will it meet your needs and will it hold up?

Many times the pre-assembled bags are reduced in cost because they have low quality items (not all, but many). Would you be happy with a multifunctioning knife you have never tried and do not know its quality or how long it will last, or would you rather have in your bag a high quality knife?

Before you spend your hard earned money, please stop, think, evaluate, and then buy what you think will be best for you and your family. Buy items you know, trust, and that you have researched out. Don't settle for less. Remember, it is **YOUR** life you are investing in. Do you want to just get by or do you want to thrive as you survive?

Learn from other's mistakes. Prepare as they did not. Do not take short cuts and do not go cheap. If you do, the only ones who will suffer will be your loved ones. Therefore, as a family, have each kit completed, make sure each item in your kit works, and that everyone including children know how to use them. Try to have multiples of the tools you will need for survival, and have backups for everything. Prepare yourself now for what you will use to help others with and determine at what point you will need to stop assisting.

Chapter 6

Question 3

Do you have food your family will actually eat and enjoy, and do you have a long term means of preparing them?

During hurricane season, you can walk into almost any store and they will have displays of items you should purchase for your relief kit. Many put out items such as rice, beans, potted meat, and cases of water. Now, I do not know about you, but I personally am not a fan of certain canned meat and would be hard pressed to consume them.

One big mistake we have seen people make over and over again is that they put into their food kits items that were cheap and things they usually did not eat. They figured the odds of something happening were slim so they were not going to waste their money but they decided to prepare something just in case. When something did happen, they found out quickly that neither they nor their children liked the food, nor did they have enough. Their decision forced them to either wait for relief supplies to be brought into their area or go searching for some.

Your neighbors may be willing to help you but (like in many areas we have responded to) they also may be in the same situation as you and most stores only have about a 3-day supply of food stock. If it takes weeks or months to get food into your area, what will you do?

The following is what you need to know and think about as you are preparing your food kit.

In disaster sites, you will see long lines of people waiting in distribution lines for food, water, and ice. Feeding stations are packed with people wanting a hot meal because they either did not have relief supplies, they hated what they stored, or they did not have a way to cook them (a very common mistake we have seen in every disaster).

We are asked all the time - Which would be better to have - canned goods, dehydrated foods, or freeze dried foods? Our answer is: all three.

There are different stages to a disaster: the initial event, post event (1-14 days), and long term recovery (months or years following the event). Actual recovery after a major event is usually months or years - not days - so be prepared for it!

Canned goods are great for the initial and post event; much of the food can be eaten without any water being required - just make sure to pack food you and your family will eat. Don't buy things you won't eat just because they are cheap!

The down side to canned goods is the weight and the expiration date. People buy canned goods and they go bad before they are ever used. Dehydrated and freeze dried foods are perfect for long-term storage and after you have a safe drinking source. (You can make sure you have a safe drinking source by having a proper filtration and purification system that we will address in a different chapter.) Another advantage to freeze dried food is that it tastes good. Freeze-dried food can be eaten right out of the can without being rehydrated. This means you do not have to have water to spare and you do not put scent up into the air that might attract other hungry people you cannot afford to feed. The beauty of freeze-dried food is that you can buy it and put it away and not worry about checking it for many, many years.

Be forewarned, not all dehydrated and freeze-dried foods are the same so do your research and try them out. My team and I tried a wide variety of products. Some we liked and some we did not. Some had long listings in their ingredients while others were just the food item itself. (When you are buying dehydrated carrots, the ingredients should be carrots not carrots plus a whole lot of other things.) There are also companies that promote gluten free but **BEWARE**! If they do not say they are **certified gluten free**, then it is not guaranteed to be gluten free. There are companies that provide good tasting, good quality, and allergy safe food. Don't settle for less because in a disaster you want good food that you will enjoy eating, and is safe for you and your family's food allergies.

One common comment we hear all the time when asking people about their relief food is that their freeze-dried or dehydrated food is "OK" – just "OK!" This can be a dangerous food supply to have because when you are working long hard days trying to rebuild after a disaster and you are exhausted at the end of the day, your initial response will be to just go to bed because you are too tired to eat. (My team and I know this first hand as we have been at this mind set on numerous occasions). It is vital during disaster time to eat especially when you are burning many calories! It is when you are tempted to just go to bed that you must force yourself to eat because if you do not, your body will not have the nutrients it needs to survive and thrive in the new environment you are living in. Lack of food will lead to fatigue, weakness, and make you more prone to illness. If your food source is just "OK," that is telling us that there is a high probability that when you drag yourself in from hard labor at the end of the day and you are too tired to eat and you just want to sleep, you will not force yourself (which you must do) to eat the food you have. You must NEVER just go to bed at the end of the day without eating unless you have no food. You MUST fight the desire to skip eating and make sure to consume the much needed and required nutrition your body needs. The only way to help this dilemma you will face is to have food you really like and enjoy. Do not settle for food that tastes just "OK." Get food you think tastes great! It really does make a difference, and you do not have to settle for less if you properly prepare now.

The downside of dehydrated and freeze-dried foods is that it can be expensive. The truth of the matter is that the price really is not bad when you consider the amount you get and the fact that it has a long shelf life. Besides that, what are you and your family worth? Invest in your future and do not cut corners.

There is another situation that happens when people do not stock food they enjoy eating or that tastes good – we call it food fatigue. When you are forced to eat the same food over and over again, you become fatigued with the taste and eventually will stop eating or greatly reduce the amount you are eating because the thought of consuming the same food item actually becomes so repulsive to you that you would prefer to starve.

This can be very dangerous, especially for children. I have had parents tell me that if their child is hungry enough they will eat but the fact is, if a child dislikes the taste they will decide to go hungry. If they get bored with the taste they will do the same thing.

In a disaster it is very important to get enough calories to keep you healthy and strong. You will have many hardships to deal with and will need all your strength.

One way to avoid food fatigue is to make sure to pack items you and your children enjoy along with seasonings so you can alter the flavor in order to have variety. It is also important to have some comfort food, especially following a disaster event. After a crisis, fear, anxiety, stress, and exhaustion are your biggest enemy. Having a comfort food will help to alleviate some of the stress while you work to find your new balance.

Remember – it is your life and you are worth every dollar you invest into it. Do not rely on someone else because no one will take better care of you and your family than you will!

WARNING - When you are dealing with a long-term disaster event, food for many is in short supply. This means that those who do not have will be searching for those who do have. When people around you start running out of food, you must stop cooking all your food and start eating your freeze-dried foods from the can or other foods you do not need to cook. Cooking food puts an aroma into the air and will attract hungry people a mile away. If you do not have the supplies to feed all your neighbors, then it is vital that they think you are in the same situation they are and you must not do anything to attract attention to yourself. If you continue to cook your food, it might result in your supplies being taken by force. Remember the Black Friday example I gave you? We have seen people fighting, and yes, even shoot others for the food they had in their hands. Therefore, keep your family and supplies safe by paying attention to the environment and conditions of those around you and respond accordingly.

One note of caution – baked apple pie candles and other deliciously smelling candles will also attract hungry people due to the fact they truly smell like food so do not burn any scented candles during a time when people are hungry. If your light source is coming from candles, make sure your candles are odorless.

To help you, we put together a list of food for one person for 4 months. This list is a guideline to get you started and help you see the type of items you should be storing. This list does not include your food for the initial stage after a disaster as you will want to eat whatever food supply you have during that time. This list addresses the food you will need for the long haul. Our team chose Thrive Life Food and the list I am providing are the items we use.

FOOD LIST FOR 1 PERSON FOR 4 MONTHS

This is a basic 4-month supply and can be altered to fit your family's needs, but remember this is a list for **ONE** person. It may seem like a lot but you will burn many calories and will need to keep up your strength. It will always be better to have too much than too little so please feel free to expand and add more if you desire. Also, many of the foods, especially the meats, cheese, and veggies can be made into a trail mix, not reconstituted, and still taste great.

2 #10 cans each of: chicken, crumbled hamburger, roast beef

1 #10 can of cheese

6 #10 cans of mashed potatoes

6 #10 cans of macaroni noodles

2 #10 cans of pancake mix

1 #10 can of eggs

1 bucket of white Rice

1 bucket cornmeal

1 bucket white flour

1 bucket of milk

6 #10 cans of vegetables such as broccoli, carrots, green beans, cauliflower, etc.

1 #10 can of butter

1 #10 can of salt

1 #10 can of baking soda

2 #10 cans pinto beans

2 #10 cans small red beans

2 #10 cans kidney beans

Each person must have at least one of the following (for a wider variety you may choose to have all of them):

EITHER

1 – #10 can chicken bouillon

OR

1 – #10 can of beef bouillon

OR

1 – #10 can of tomato powder

NEXT:

Each person must have at least one of the following:

EITHER

1 can of honey crystals

OR

1 can of brown sugar

OR

1 can of peanut butter powder

For every two people in your family or group you should have:

1 bucket of cane sugar

For a treat, consider having a few #10 cans of fruit and #10 cans of either chocolate milk or hot cocoa mix. Though fruit and chocolate milk is not essential, it will add a variety to your meals and a pick

Chapter 7

Question 4

Do you have supplies for a minimum of 2 weeks?

A disaster or crisis can last for many months and years, not just days. Have you ever heard about any major disaster that actually only lasted a couple of days? I haven't. Yet, each year when the public is reminded to prepare for hurricanes or tornadoes, they are only told by certain public agencies to have a 2-3 day supply kit!

We have never been in any major (or minor for that matter) disaster event that had complete recovery within 2-3 days. We recommend that at bare minimum you have at least a 2-week relief plan with supplies, but ideally your minimum should be 2 months and grow from there. We have been in areas where life did not return to normal for years.

Have you ever stopped to think what you would do if, in an instant, you lost everything including all the common comforts and luxuries we acquired over the past 200 or more years? Have you thought about how you will respond, or how your family will survive if it takes years to rebuild?

During Katrina, months after the storm ravished the coastline; we were still doing distribution and aid work to the people there. They still had no usable water, electric, or housing, and most lost all they owned. Essential supplies were hard to come by, and people were so desperate they would take whatever they could get to help meet a need.

During one of our response trips, we were taking supplies to a location called "Tent City." It was a location set up to house the people who had lost everything. It was rows of tents set up for shelter and lodging for those in need. People from all walks of life – wealthy and poor alike found themselves in the same situation and had to rely on the generosity of others not affected by the storm.

A request was sent out to the non-profits for clothing so we brought in a truck load of clothing and distributed them to the people who lined up and received needed clothing according to their size. By the time one man got to the head of the line, he needed any warm clothing we had as the temperature was starting to get colder. We were completely out of men's clothing and the only thing we had were some women's bright pink and purple sweaters and long shirts. His response was, "That will work, I am cold and I do not care what I wear as long as it will keep me warm."

I know it is hard for people to comprehend that thought because we live such blessed and protected lives. We are not faced with war and daily devastation. When we see storm ravaged towns far away from us, we cannot begin to understand what they are going through, and we reassure ourselves that it will never happen to us. Please understand, that is a lie of comfort you are feeding yourself. It is important you absorb, understand, and accept the fact that bad things do happen and can happen anywhere at any time including your neighborhood and the best way to make it easier is to take the time and prepare now.

You need to look at and evaluate things from a realistic standpoint. If you live far away from any large town and a disaster hits, there is a high probability that you will not get assistance quickly as most relief agencies respond to large population areas first. (We are an agency that responds to smaller population areas first and work our way inward, but we are the exception, not the norm.) Relief supplies are abundant at the onset in many areas but diminish quickly. No relief agency has enough supplies to help everyone, nor do they have enough to assist you through an entire crisis period. You must determine what you want now: do you want to be self-sufficient or dependent? A self-sufficient family does not prepare a 2-3 day relief kit to survive any type of disaster. A self-sufficient family prepares with game plans, supplies, skills, tools, and connections to survive indefinitely. Why? Because they determined that they will take responsibility and learn all they need to know such as homesteading skills, medical and alternative medical options, necessary survival skills, and have set aside relief supplies such as food, seeds, etc.

This book will not help you prepare your kits (as I have stated before) because I already wrote *Preparation Made Simple* to help you accomplish that. But this section is here to make you aware that you need to have at least 2 months (2 months should be your beginning point, not your ending point) set aside to make the burden easier for you if a crisis should hit.

During one of the conventions I was speaking at, a gentleman and his family came up to speak to me. He told me he had recently lost his job but that they were doing well – why –

because he set aside 6 months of relief supplies and cash in the event a major crisis happened. Little did he know that the crisis would be a job loss.

He proceeded to tell me the one area they were not prepared in was medical and that was why they were there. He heard about what we taught in natural alternatives and the kits we had, and the whole family came to learn.

Disaster or crisis can come in many different forms. For this family, they were weathering it beautifully because they prepared. Preparation does not have to be a doom and gloom conspiracy theory topic but it is one of personal responsibility.

The more you do now the easier life can be later!

Chapter 8

Question 5

Do you have all your paperwork in order – including that which you will need to reenter your area after an evacuation?

The Documents kit is the most dreaded kit of all because it can be time consuming and tedious, but it is a very important part of your relief supplies! If you do not take time to put together all your important documentation now, you will be highly challenged if a major disaster of any type hits.

After a disaster, you must be able to prove you are who you say you are. You will need to be able to show ownership of your home, a rental, your vehicle, insurance, and you will want your medical records in the event of a medical emergency.

The largest mistake we see in this area of preparation is - most people have no documentation at all!

Medical Records

Let's start with your medical records. If you are forced to evacuate and you or a family member have any medical condition you are being treated for, it will be important for you to have documentation proving it. You will also need to prove who has been treating you, what medication you are on, or what treatments you have been receiving. If you do not, your treatment may be greatly delayed and your medication may not be refilled.

In one major disaster we worked, people evacuated all over the country and most of those people did not have medical records. We were brought in to help several families – some with heart issues, others with cancer, COPD, and ADD. Unfortunately, none of these people had medical records and were angry because they went to a hospital or clinic and were not receiving immediate care for their conditions, but none of them had documentation to prove they had their stated illness. The medical facilities they went to could not just take their word for it.

Research into their condition had to be done, attempts to locate and speak with their existing doctors, new tests, etc. The evacuees were angry because they wanted their care without interruption but their lack of preparedness caused the delay, not the attending medical professionals. The doctors and nurses were just doing their jobs. So must you. Take time to compile all your important medical information. You do not need documentation for every time you had a cold but you will need it for the current medication you are on or any regimented treatment plan you are undergoing. In the event you have to evacuate and go to a medical complex that is not familiar with you, your treatment and care will not be hindered or delayed. Make sure to have everyone's shot records in your kits. (We will address later what happens when the disaster is so large that there may not be any medical care available for you).

Proof of Residency

During all the disasters we worked on in the United States, this paperwork was needed when either an evacuation had been enforced and you wanted to return home, or an event happened (such as a tornado) and those who lived in the affected area wanted to get in to see if family, friends, their animals, and their homes survived.

When the National Guard, police agencies, or other units are established and form a road block to protect the area that has been devastated or affected, they will not allow anyone in who is not able to prove they reside in that location. If the area has been damaged and is deemed unsafe, you will not get back in until the all clear is given for returning residents. When they do allow people back in, you will need a current utility bill with your address on it in order to get in. This requirement prevents the curious onlookers from getting into the disaster zone and getting in the way. It also helps prevent increased injuries from people who have no business being there. We have seen many people make the mistake of not having a bill to show residency because they figured their driver's license would be sufficient, but in most cases it is not. The reason behind this is because people move all the time and do not change the address on their license. What was occurring in disaster areas were former residents who had not changed the address on their driver's license were using it to get into the area just to see the damage – not to help – but just to watch, see, and take pictures!

Understand that getting through a check point may take hours so be prepared to wait in a long line of others wanting to get home. Realize that if you do not have sufficient paperwork to prove you live in the area being blocked off, you will be turned away and not let in until they open the area up to the general public. The individuals working at the checkpoint must follow orders and if they are told to only let people in who have a current utility bill and a picture ID, you will not be getting in if you do not have what they require!

Insurance Information

I wish I had good news in this area but I do not!

If you have insurance and need to file a claim do not expect it to go quickly. Sometimes, depending on where you live (large city or small town), insurance companies may set up a central point for you to stand in line to file a claim which could take hours to just get through the line. Then there is the paper work and the long wait to get compensated.

If you have ever had to submit an insurance claim for anything, did it go quickly? Now imagine your insurance company is being hit for thousands of requests at one time. How quickly do you think it will go now?

You will not be able to make them move faster through the thousands of claims being filed, but you can make sure you have everything you need ahead of time to assist approval of your claim by having all necessary documentation. Have before and after pictures; have itemized information on contents of your home; make sure you know in detail what your insurance will cover. If you live in a flood-prone area, make sure you have flood insurance!

Other Important Documentation

Other important documentation you will want to have are birth certificates, marriage certificate, driver license, phone numbers of all credit card companies, life insurance, important phone numbers, and social security numbers.

Information on life insurance, social security, etc. is important to have in the event you or a family member does not survive. Having this information will help when it is requested by different agencies attempting to help. If you are retired military, make sure to have your DD-214.

Having phone numbers for credit card companies will assist you by allowing you to contact them immediately after an event. Many companies will wave payments for a certain amount of time for disaster victims. It is their way of helping those in the crisis area.

Your document kit will benefit you greatly if you are a victim in a disaster area by making sure you have the proper identification, paperwork, medical history, and account numbers you will need to file most claims or to get proper assistance with whatever needs you may have.

It is a tough kit for many to assemble but, when disaster strikes, you will be thankful you took the time and got it done!

Chapter 9

Question 6

Do you think you are indestructible?

It is human nature to think, "It will never happen to me." After all, we tend to see ourselves as indestructible.

People jump out of airplanes with a parachute on their back, they run off the sides of mountains to hang glide, or leap off sides of tall bridges with only a bungee cord to keep them from hitting the ground – a little extreme you might say. OK then, let's try this – we mow our yards without protective eye gear because we know flying debris only hits other people in the eyes, not us; we move rusty metal or other yard debris with no gloves because we will be careful so we won't get cut because only others get cut, not us; in the south we walk through the grass in our bare feet where snakes are known to roam because we know we won't get bitten until it actually does happen. When it does we are stunned and confused and ask ourselves "how in the world did that happen to me". The list goes on and on. We take so many things for granted and we always believe the bad things will not happen to us, only to others.

When a disaster happens in your area, it happens to everyone but injuries do not have to since many can be prevented. After an event, people attempt to do things the way they always have. They do not think about injuries from cleanup because they never thought about them before-hand.

The fact is, many injuries occur after a disaster event during the clean-up process, a time when you really cannot afford to have even a minor accident. Flying debris and contaminated water splashing into your eyes can be prevented with proper eyewear. Severe cuts and limb loss can be prevented with proper boots and work gloves. Getting cut on a normal day is not enjoyable and considered an inconvenience, but being cut in a disaster site where there are many dangerous bacteria and lack of medical assistance can prove to be a hardship beyond your wildest imagination.

Our goal is to help you be prepared in all areas of life and encourage you to think about the value of that which each one of us takes for granted each day.

In a disaster, you cannot afford to have any type of injury, especially broken bones, cut hands or feet, or eye injuries. Sometimes we cannot prevent something from happening but many times we can by simply using good common sense and having good protective gear. A strong pair of work gloves, safety glasses, and work boots will protect you from many injuries and are a MUST in your disaster relief supplies. Buy the best quality protective gear you can because it will be something you will rely on greatly after the storm. Once you buy them, start using them! By doing this you are protecting yourself from known hazards that cause numerous injuries every year AND you will be forming a habit so when a disaster does strike it will be natural to put the protective gear on.

If you do not use the gear now, odds are you will not think to use it in a disaster because your mindset will be the same as it always has been – "only other people get hurt – not me!"

We have seen people injured because they did not stop and think before they did something. They did not use common sense, and they did nothing to protect themselves.

If you read *Preparation Made Simple* or other articles we have written, you know we encourage you and your family to practice simple skills to help you through any crisis. Learning to wear protective gear is a skill many must practice because few of us use it in our daily lives. It may sound silly but it is true!

Please remember this; no one – including you – is indestructible! Having the mindset that you are indestructible could prove very costly and is certainly not a lesson you want to learn in a disaster site.

Changing the way you think and creating important habits you will follow in a disaster area will make a big difference on how you come through the event!

Chapter 10

Question 7

Are You Able to Take Care of Most Medical Situations?

[Note: Before I begin this section, I must put in the disclaimer that this section has not been evaluated or approved by any medical authority or the FDA. I am not treating, diagnosing, or prescribing. I am simply telling you what others or I chose to do. What you choose to do is strictly your choice.]

Unless you are a doctor, nurse, or someone who has studied alternatives for years, your answer to the above question should be NO!

People who are preparing for disasters try to put together a medical kit or spend a lot of money on pre-assembled medical bags with items such as sutures, casting supplies, burn creams, etc. but most who buy them do not even open up the bags to see what is in them. Worse than that, they receive no training on how or when to use them. Yet when I ask them if they are prepared for most medical emergencies, their answer is always the same, "Yes, I bought a medical kit."

Owning a medical kit does not make you prepared. It will help you with the bumps, bruises, and minor scratches, and give you a false sense of preparedness, but it certainly will not help you with major cuts, broken bones, blocked airways, asthma attacks, contagious diseases such as cholera, etc.

If you have a casting kit but have never been taught how and when to use it (all broken bones do not need casting as splinting may be better), those items in your possession are useless to you unless you happen to have a friend with medical skills, or you choose to use it as a bartering item.

Today, medical skills are available to the common person because there are several doctors who will now teach you the necessary survival medical skills you need. It is not free but it is well worth the money for you to learn these life saving techniques. However, what is most important that you understand is that you will more likely have to deal with infections, illnesses, and disease than you will have to suture or cast a broken bone. So I will be addressing both in greater detail.

Yes, you can learn to suture, skin staple, diagnose a problem, cast, splint, help an asthmatic even if there is no electricity, know how to handle a cholera outbreak, venomous snake bites, bullet wounds, etc. If you do not learn these skills, what will you do if someone is stabbed, shot, bit by a rabid animal, gets heat stroke, a heart attack, or some other medical emergency that your store bought bag is not equipped to remedy for you?

One thing I have seen and learned over the past 18 major disasters that we responded to is that for the most part, people are unable to take care of themselves from a medical point of view.

We, as a people, have for so long relied on others to tell us what we need to do where our health is concerned instead of taking a proactive role like our great-grandparents used to do. "Way back when" they had to know how to help themselves because medical services were not always readily available. That meant that most knew about and used such alternatives as homeopathy, herbs, essential oils, and grandma's little known remedies. They also knew how to take care of cuts, wounds, sprains, and broken bones.

Today, few people know all the benefits of these old traditional remedies and skills but instead visit their doctors on a regular basis. Now I am not telling you to stop going to the doctor, but I am suggesting that you start learning the many alternative options you have available to you, so if a crisis or disaster leaves you without medical assistance, you will not be rendered totally helpless.

My family used to go to the doctor for ear infections and sore throats but learned through our research (and practicing what we learned) that we could take care of these illnesses simply by using natural alternatives. We know how to truly protect ourselves against the "common bugs" that attack people each year causing so many to become ill, but if someone does get sick, we also know how to help them through natural options. We learned how to take care of various and potentially debilitating wounds, how to help someone having breathing problems, and a wide range of other health issues including infections and diseases. By learning and practicing these skills, we are strengthening our ability to help ourselves when a disaster happens and modern medicine is not available. An added bonus is that it also improves our ability to help ourselves on a daily basis.

When disaster strikes and you are in a die or try situation, the more options and determination you have will help you weather the storm. Just like relief kits are an important part of preparedness, so are the skills that you acquire.

More and more people are taking medical training to help themselves and their loved ones in the event of a disaster. We highly recommend you do as well if you have not. One skill many people are learning is how to suture. We also believe this is a great skill to have. While it is easy to find places to go to learn to suture, many of those places do not teach skin stapling which is also an excellent skill to have in the event of a disaster. What you must understand is that many cuts and lacerations will be best left unsutured. By taking a training course on how to do this, you will also learn how to properly clean and determine which ones need suturing or stapling and which ones need to be left open.

In the event a surface wound needs to be closed, skin stapling is fast and efficient. It takes only seconds to do and can be done without a numbing agent, reducing the distress and discomfort to the patient. Suturing, if it is actually needed, will take longer and if you have no numbing agent, will be distressing to both you and the loved one you are assisting. This would be an action you should take if you are in a die or try situation and you are the only medical care around. If medical care is within reach, properly clean the wound, cover, and get help.

I was once asked to evaluate a family's relief kits and preparedness skills. In doing so, I found out that their medical training came from watching an online video, and their suturing kit was their grandma's very old needle and thread kit – neither received a good mark from me! They did not want to pay for proper medical training so I informed them about skin stapling - a much better choice than their chosen game plan.

Our team knows both skills – suturing and stapling. My first choice is stapling because of the ease and speed at which it can be done. It also comes ready to go so it requires little preparation time or stillness of hand. If needed, you could do it on yourself.

Should you only learn to skin staple – no, because staples cannot be used for everything. However, when it can be used and you know how to do it, you will be grateful to have that option over just suturing.

I teach people not to put all their eggs into one basket and to make their relief kits and skills as well rounded as possible. By learning both suturing and skin stapling and the proper way to use both, you have more options if a disaster strikes. Remember: One is none!

But what if you do not know either of these skills and you find yourself in a medical emergency with no one to assist you? Do not panic; remain calm, and think. You have an open wound that needs to be well cleaned out, disinfected, and closed. What do you have on hand? If all you have is raw honey, duct tape, and gauze, could you help the injured person? I am not allowed to give medical recommendations so I leave you with that scenario and encourage you to learn the answer. When presented with an emergency, remember it is critically important to remain calm so you can think through all your options and handle it the best way possible with what is available to you.

During the last disaster we responded to, like so many others, we encountered too many people who were sick and distressed because their doctors' offices and pharmacies were closed and hospital services were not available to them. They were miserable and suffering with the belief there were no options. Every person we worked with, except one, could have helped themselves if they had known about natural alternatives, had some basic skills, or had taken the time to think of actual options they did have. Please do not wait until it is too late – start learning now. The more you know, the better the chances you have to be able to help yourself and your loved ones if something terrible should happen. If no crisis ever occurs, you still have learned important skills you can use to improve your own health and well-being with nothing lost but much gained!

If you go into most homes, you will see that many have quite the medicine cabinet for that "just in the event" moment – someone gets a sore throat, a headache, an upset stomach, insomnia, a flesh wound, etc. Few, however, have an old time cabinet like their great grandparents used to have that included safe, all natural remedies for when someone got a sore throat, a headache, an upset stomach, insomnia, a flesh wound, etc. What is the difference between the two? The first one was all purchased; whether it was over-the-counter or by prescription. Many have side effects and you cannot make them yourself. Our great-grandparent's cabinets were filled with many of the same useful remedies – ones they either learned to make themselves or they purchased from someone who knew how to make them. However, their cabinet was backed up by skills that were taught to them for how to tend to injuries and illnesses, and wise useful tips and ideas.

I am not a big proponent on pre-assembled medical bags as so many of them are over expensive, and stuffed full of fluff (plain regular bandages, cotton balls, and creams) you could easily purchase yourself. They rarely have the products you will need in a disaster area unless you are preparing for just the minor issues.

If you take the time to assemble your own medical kits, you can save money and have good quality, and essential alternatives to help you with whatever medical crisis comes along. If you have ever attended one of my trainings, you heard me say, "If you are in a die or try situation, you better try because dying should not be an option."

Many people in America still do not believe in alternatives, but if you are the only person around to help injured people after a major disaster, you will want all the options available to use in order to have the best outcome. Traditional medical is important to have, but you will not have medicine to help someone bitten by a rabid animal or for an epidemic, but if you know alternatives, you have a chance of helping them. You will need to have the knowledge and the skill set to assist them, or you may just have to watch them die.

Please know, not everyone you try to help may live, but wouldn't it be better to try than to just sit by and let them die not doing anything. I can tell you for those who sat by helpless, the guilt and memory of that tragic moment in time remains with them; usually forever.

I want to side step just a moment onto a very important topic about contagious and infectious disease after a disaster. I wrote an article on this topic after the Ebola outbreak and am inserting it into this book for your information. You must understand that after a disaster, the bacteria count sky rockets, and even a minor cut can turn into a life threating situation. What you think is a cold or a simple case of diarrhea, could actually be the beginnings of a potential epidemic – something you certainly want to avoid at all cost if possible. So here is what you need to know, not just for times of disaster, but for everyday life:

Every year we have infectious and contagious illnesses that go around such as the yearly flu bug, a stomach virus, chickenpox, or even the common cold. An infectious illness is not always highly contagious. Although some contagious illnesses are just irritations, others can be deadly and it pays to have a plan on how you will address them.

Not long ago, we heard about Ebola, something no one ever expected to be a problem in our country. It is something no one wants to get, and everyone wanted to know how to protect themselves from it. Though Ebola is an infectious disease, it is not considered to be a highly contagious disease, due to the way the virus is spread. In this case, it is through contact with the bodily fluid of an infected person, or touching something the infected person has touched.

During times of disaster, many sicknesses and diseases can break out causing great hardship on those who must endure it. The specific illness and condition of the person who is infected will determine their outcome. It is important to understand potential illnesses, and how to handle them. Cholera is an illness that is a potential threat after major events when water becomes contaminated, and people accidentally consume the bacteria. (Food washed with the contaminated water and then consumed will also potentially make a person sick.) Long duration disaster or social break down could lead to illnesses we have not seen in this country for a long time (if ever). Take time to learn about Typhus, Typhoid Fever, Smallpox, and Rabies so you know or have a better understanding of what they are, their symptoms, and alternative options for dealing with them if professional medical help is not available for you or you choose not to go the traditional medical route. You may not know what is making a person sick but there are many things you can do to educate and protect yourself before, during, and after an event, or just during your everyday life.

It is important to know that a virus or bacteria can be spread in different ways. Some are airborne, so they are passed on by coughing or sneezing (this form of spreading is considered highly contagious). Others are spread through bodily fluid, and picked up by exposure – after you touch something a sick person touched and then eat food or rub your eyes or nose without washing your hands after coming in contact with the germ.

There are steps a person can take to improve their chances of not getting an illness but it requires changes on the part of each individual.

This next paragraph may seem a little tedious or frivolous, but bear with me because it really is important, especially after a crisis.

The first important step in protecting yourself is to wash your hands! Many people go through the day, and never wash their hands. They get on buses, touch public door handles, use public restrooms, go shopping and use shopping carts, handle money, and yet, they do not take the time to wash – I mean *really* wash their hands. Just running your hands underwater does not clean them; it simply wets them. You must use soap. Lather the soap on your hands, scrub, and rinse. (One Certified Nursing Assistant program recommends singing "Twinkle, Twinkle, Little Star" or "The Alphabet Song" to yourself while scrubbing with soap to ensure you do so for the proper amount of time to actually disinfect.) A common mistake after washing is to retouch, with your clean hand, the dirty faucet you just turned on, which in turn will re-expose you to the germs you just rinsed down the drain. The safe way after washing your hands is to grab a paper towel and use it to turn the water off and then another clean towel to dry your hands. Do not grab the door handle when you walk out the door because not everyone washes their hands, and then you are exposing yourself to the same germs you just got rid of! So now you may be thinking – "Just how are we supposed to do this after a disaster?" Reality is, for a time you may not be able to, and *that is the point*. Most people make it a habit not to do those things now, so they most certainly will not think to do it after a major event when their body is exposed to many *more dangerous* germs than they are used to, leaving them susceptible to all sorts of illnesses. After an event, when safe water is not available, it will be important to take other steps to protect yourself such as faithfully disinfecting with several types of disinfectants such as vodka, essential oils, and colloidal silver, wearing gloves or masks, and boosting your immune system. It will also require you to remember not to touch your eyes, mouth, or ears, not to eat anything until you have properly washed, cover your mouth when you cough and your nose when you sneeze, and avoid others who may be sick! These are habits that need to be instilled in each family member or team member now!

It seems like a lot of work but when you are trying to avoid an illness, it requires conscious and deliberate work on your part. Some people make the mistake of thinking they can just use hand disinfectant all the time instead of washing, but that does not kill every germ, bacteria, or virus. Once a safe water source is secured, diligently follow proper hand washing to protect yourself and those around you, and insist they do the same!

Is it more work? Of course. But does it protect you? **YES**!

Become aware of what you touch around you and how many times you rub your face or eat without washing. Sorry, there is no such thing as a "3-second rule". This was verified by "Myth Busters". Also, pay attention to how many people cough or sneeze around you without covering their mouth or nose as well as those who do cover their mouth with their hand when they cough or sneeze and then touch something right after the fact (like offering to shake your hand).

Avoiding a virus or bacteria means you must practice proper hygiene! Now is the time to get your family and your team practicing because after a disaster happens, people will do what they normally do. The problem is, after a disaster you do not know if someone who becomes sick is dealing with a life threatening illness or just an everyday common bug. After a disaster, you need to treat every illness as a potential plague in order to protect the team. Trust us. You cannot afford to have even one man down when you are trying to survive. We know this first hand!

If an infectious virus is airborne, you need to take extra precaution with a mask which most resist. Studies were done on the benefit of mask wearing to prevent the spread of a disease. They concluded that when used correctly, masks are highly effective in preventing the spread of infections, family members cut their risk of getting the flu by 70 percent when they washed their hands often and wore surgical masks, and the use of masks should always be paired with regular hand washing.

In earlier times when someone was sick, they were quarantined, a practice rarely used today. People send their children to school sick, they go to work sick, they go shopping while they are sick, etc. which means they are exposing people to the illness everywhere they go and the next thing you know, we have an epidemic.

In a disaster situation, you want to practice quarantine because you will not be able to afford an epidemic. Quarantining one person to prevent the spread of an illness is much better than everyone becoming sick.

Some of you are going to hate this next statement but it needs to be said. Another step you can take now to help yourself is to boost your immune system. People with a weak or compromised immune system are more likely to get sick than someone with a strong healthy immune system. To help improve your immune system, you need to eat well, exercise, get enough rest, and consider taking supplements since most people do not consume enough of the proper nutrients to give their bodies everything they need. I know, this is something many of you hear from your doctor all the time but you really need to be in the best shape and health of your life to have the best options and endurance that will be required from you after a storm or disaster event of any kind.

Historically, people used homeopathy, essential oils, herbs, minerals, and raw honey to help themselves and their families before, and during times of crisis. In more recent times people also turned to newer alternatives such as colloidal silver and meso silver. Even though these have been available a long time, they are not as popular as the homeopathic, herbs, etc.

Part of being healthy and to help yourself if you become ill is to know your options. On the website for The National Center for Homeopathy, you can learn what homeopathy is and how it has been used historically as a preventative and as an option if one becomes ill. At the time of this writing, according to the World Health Organization, homeopathy is the second largest medical system for primary care in the world and warrants looking into when you are looking for options to protect yourself against getting sick or you are preparing your emergency relief kits. (If you would like more information, you can go to our website and read about homeopathy – what it is and how it can help you. Because we know the important value of homeopathy, we also created a kit we use when we go into disaster areas. Information about our kits is also on our website.)

Herbs and essential oils have also been used throughout the generations with great success. You would be wise to educate yourself on the value and benefits of both of them. Be forewarned, you will need to take the time to research the different herbs. You may want to use and learn about the potential side effects and contraindications some have because not every person can take every herb, and therefore, it is not our first alternative choice. If you choose to educate yourself on herbs, learn to identify them in nature and learn which ones are indigenous to your area.

One way I recommend to start learning how to identify the different herbs is to purchase a medicinal heirloom herbal seed kit and start growing them in your home as houseplants. You will see what each plant looks like at its different stages of its life and you will be better equipped to recognize it in nature. You will also want to take a class or buy a good book on how to dry your herbs, how to re-harvest your seeds for future planting, and what part of the herb is used for medicinal purposes.

If you are looking into essential oils, then you must know that not all oils are created equal and not all oils can be used for health benefits. (We have articles about this topic on our website as well.)

Other alternatives my family has used, and we keep in our relief kit is raw honey, (which has so many benefits and uses that this item should not be overlooked as an essential option in your kits) and colloidal and meso silver.

Now before you close your mind to colloidal silver as an alternative, it warrants your investigation into it, however, do not buy into the lie that it will turn you blue. That was proven to be false. The person who turned blue was not using a true form of colloidal silver. If you want to make this a tool in your kit read "The Truth about Silver Protein Products" before making your selection.

By practicing good hygiene, avoiding areas where sick people congregate, learning alternatives, and working on your own health now, you can improve your chance of not getting sick with whatever may be going around.

As a crisis first responder during disasters, we cannot express the importance of all these steps. During a disaster you will be exposed to a high level of germs and bacteria you are not usually exposed to, and all the steps above will be critical to your well-being. Knowing alternative options on potential ways to help you are also crucial in the event medical care is not available and is unlikely to become available to you for some time. (For more information on homeopathy or other alternatives and their benefits during time of crisis, visit our website at tradingpostinthewoods.com).

Remember - Knowledge is Power and a Key to Success.

Chapter 11

Question 8

Do you plan on just living off the land?

When talking with people about their disaster relief plans, time and time again, we are told – "No problem, if some major crisis hits, I am heading for the woods and will live off the land."

Some people may laugh at that response, others will agree with it because it is their plan as well, and there are those of us who will look at them and let them know – it's just not as easy as you think!

People have a false belief that they will be able to exit a populated city, and head for the woods where they will be able to enjoy a comfortable life while riding out whatever crisis is affecting the country. They look at it like a vacation and an adventure all rolled into one. They do not logically think it out and realize the dangers and hardships they will actually encounter. They do not think about the thugs, the wild animals, snakes, biting insects, daily food, water, etc. They forget, or do not realize that most of the people living in the city have the same game plan and the same skills as they do, which for most amounts to very little. There **WILL** be a mass exodus from the larger populated areas with everyone trying to find their piece of the woods to live in. Most of the evacuees from the cities will have no game plan or knowledge on how to survive.

There is a lot that goes into just "Living off the land," especially when your life is at stake. If you do not know what you are doing, you could find yourself in a world of trouble. Your lack of knowledge, skill set (it requires a lot of skills to just "live off the land") and preparedness will most likely render you a casualty.

Many times we hear people say they will just hunt for food (while they are of course just "living off the land") yet they do not own a rifle, shot gun, bow and arrows, traps, etc. They have never been hunting before, nor do they know how to clean or prepare the meat they caught; and yet, in their mind – it's simple! They believe when the time comes, they will just do it, and all will go perfectly well for them.

They do not understand they will no longer have a grocery store to go buy food, no ketchup and mustard for their burgers unless they know how to make it themselves, no bread and butter, or chocolate desserts. It means if they are lucky and have a rifle or shot gun, they will be spending potentially hours or days seeking an animal they can shoot, while trying to avoid everyone else who is on the hunt. If they do kill or trap an animal, they will have to clean it properly so as not to make everyone ill. After they clean the animal, they then will have to cook it so they also need to know how to start a fire. But then the aroma from their new catch, hopefully properly prepared, will attract many other hungry people who will want to eat what they caught, even if it means taking it by force.

The mindset that you will evacuate to the woods and just hunt for all your food and live happily ever after is a potential disaster and is truly a denial of the truth!

The truth is that there is much to learn about "living off the land" and it does not just happen successfully overnight without any tools or skills.

The Pilgrims came to a new land thinking they could make a go of it, but until the Indians stepped in and assisted and taught them, they struggled and many died. The American settlers who moved out of the cities on the East coast to the prairie land of the West also encountered great perils and hardships, and relied heavily on the experiences and teachings of those who had previously survived the move and established their new homesteads.

Whenever you are taking on a new adventure, it is important to learn the necessary skills required to succeed. Rarely is it a good idea to head out blindly with the hope that all will be "just fine".

If you are planning on hunting wildlife for your sources of food, then you need to have the right equipment, know how to shoot, trap, track, and prepare what you caught.

When someone tells me they will go into the woods and just plant a garden I know the odds of their success are slim to none unless they know the soil content and have what is needed to enrich it for proper vegetation growth. In a series that I have been working on, my family and I purchased wilderness land and we labored for over a year to get just a small section of the ground ready for growing crops effectively. We had to remove all the trees and brush by hand and then build up the soil so edible plants could grow. We worked many long, hard hours to learn what we would need to do so we would be properly prepared if we ever had to just "live off the land."

Do you have Heirloom seeds, and everything you need to make the garden flourish? Store bought seeds that are not heirloom will not allow you to re-harvest the seeds for future crops. If you do have heirloom seeds, do you know how to properly harvest and store your seeds for future planting? When I am evaluating people on their preparedness skills, many do not even think about gardening as a skill, but more like a hobby that can be picked up at any time. Most people purchased a seed kit but have never tried gardening before. When I ask them about harvesting seeds, they reply, "Why do I need to know how to do that?" The simple answer to that question is because if you do not know how to re-harvest your seeds, eventually you will run out, and then what are you going to plant for food? Gardening and harvesting seeds is an essential skill you must know if you plan to survive. I encourage people to purchase good quality heirloom seed kits from reputable companies.

[Note: I personally use seeds from White Harvest Seeds. I am not getting money to promote them in this book. I am sharing their name with you because I believe in the quality of their seeds and the work they are doing to help people learn how to garden.]

Once you have your seeds and a place to grow them, you must ask yourself these questions:

- Do you have the tools to dig up the roots and other trees growing in the area so that your plants can get sufficient sunlight and have enough space, soil, and nutrients to grow without having to compete with the other wild plants that may choke them out?

- Do you have natural fertilizer and other nutrients to help your plants flourish?
- Do you know how to take the new seeds and store them for future crops?
- Do you know how to dehydrate, root cellar, or preserve the food you harvest to get them through the winter?
- Do you have a way to protect your garden from bugs, insects, other critters and people who may want to eat what you planted?

The list of challenges of just "living off the land" is a long one that could go on and on: What will you do for shelter, security, medical, water, etc.? If you plan on leaving your home to just "Live off the land," you need to address all these issues before you just take off into the great outdoors. All of these topics can be managed and learned if you take the time to do it now, but unlikely if you wait until your life depends on it.

Let's take a moment to address your shelter. When I talk to people who are going to just head into the woods and live, they plan on camping. They tell me they will pitch a tent (which some who have made this their game plan do not even own). If this is your plan, do you know how to camp in a survival or disaster situation? Survival camping is not like being on a fun family vacation, but rather camping when others need what you have and are willing to do anything to get it.

We teach a survival training camp and the first thing people learn is the importance of where to place their tents. Most people will choose a convenient location, but if it is convenient for you it also means it is convenient for anyone who wants to rob you as well. They learn the importance of protecting what they have as well as themselves because people and all their belongings do become prey. We teach techniques and skills you will absolutely need if you are planning on making survival camping your plan of living during a major crisis. You need to get out of the mindset of taking a luxury camping trip and into that of emergency survival.

Reading about skills is important, but in order to know that you can actually perform them means you must put down the book and get out into the fields or wilderness and make it a part of your life.

Most people lost, or never knew, the basic skills of daily survival that our great-grandparents did. When disaster struck, our great-grandparents knew how to take care of themselves. We must become the generation that re-learns those skills, and then teaches it to the next generation.

We should never become so comfortable with modern technology that we dismiss the necessity of those basic, important life sustaining and life-saving skills.

"Living off the land" is hard work and is not accomplished overnight. Those who learn and practice now will have a better chance of survival than those who head off in an emergency into the woods for the very first time totally unprepared!

Chapter 12

Question 9

Life Without Electronics – What will you do?!!!!!!!!!!!!

Here is a challenge – tell your family that this weekend you are going to try something new – no electronics of any kind. If their response is YES, they should handle the lack of electronic devises just fine during a disaster. If their response is – WHAT? ARE YOU KIDDING? NO WAY!!! - You have a problem like millions of families around the world.

What happens when your teenager or child's cell phone or game unit does not work? For most in this day and age, their response is – I will just die!

As most of you know, we have become a civilization addicted to the wonderful conveniences of electronics; whether it is our phone, tablet, game units, computer, or television.

We have been approached by many parents who are concerned that if a disaster happens, their children will be rendered useless because they will have lost their security blanket – their electronic device! We listen to these parents talk about how their child's phone goes everywhere with them. They are constantly using them texting back and forth with their friends, even while they are eating, dressing, and watching TV. When I suggest they start breaking their child of the habit they reply – "Oh, they will never go for that, it would kill them!" First – You are the parent. Second – It will not kill them. Third – it will do them good!

I have been in disaster areas where adults asked me to please make their children get up and help them. They refuse to work because they are too upset their cell phones do not work and they cannot text their friends. They complain it is hot outside and they do not want to work. They just want to watch TV or play a computer game. Honestly, if you have this problem at your house now and you do not break the lazy addictive attitude, then you are really going to have a problem when a disaster hits. It is not my job to make your children help you.

We have seen in disaster sites where teenagers really struggle because they are lost without their electronics. Without their electronics, they cannot function. They see it as their lifeline to those they care about. They are overwhelmed and need to talk to their friends and become angry because they are not able to. They have problems focusing because they can't text. They do not want to do physical labor because they have never had to.

Unfortunately, we also see the young children struggling because they are used to having their television or game units to entertain them and now are uncertain of what to do. Even the parents have a hard time because many of them are just as addicted as their children.

If you are one of these families, we challenge you to start making a change. One night or one day a week, plan for family time. Start communicating with each other. Make everyone put down their electronics, including you, and play a board game, build Legos, go outside and have a BBQ and talk to each other, or go for a family bike ride. Just remember, it will be hard – no phones, no tablets, no TV's, no computers or other handheld devices! Once you all can give them up for a few hours, try a whole weekend! It will not be as easy as you think, but you will feel liberated when you do. It seems silly that having to go without electronics would stress people out, but it really does.

Trust us when we tell you – there are enough hardships that you will have to face during and after a disaster happens but electronic withdrawal does not have to be one of them. Neither does getting your hands dirty for the first time. If you start breaking the habit now, your whole family will work better together as a team and accomplish so much more.

Chapter 13

Question #10

Are you mentally and emotionally prepared for a disaster survival situation?

My best guess for most people is No. It is easy to say, "sure I am prepared to handle whatever comes along" but that statement for most people is spoken out of ignorance.

Fear, anxiety, high terror situations, and dealing with the unknown can be paralyzing for many normal people. That is why preparing mentally now is so important to your game plan.

On any given day, a person can lose a loved one. When that happens, they must work to overcome their pain and sorrow and find the will and the strength to carry on. Now imagine you lose your loved one (a spouse or child) during a disaster. Are your ready to cope with the loss, provide emotional support for the loved ones who survived, as well as cope with the massive destruction that may have taken place during the disaster? Not only must you be prepared mentally to deal with the loss of life, but you will also need to direct, orchestrate, and carry out your survival/relief plan that you prepared if the rest of you are going to survive.

Mentally, most of us are **NOT** prepared, nor do we want to acknowledge the thought of anyone dying so we put that thought somewhere deep in the recesses of our brain and determine to handle it when the time comes.

We also do not want to think about the fact that there are people in our world that would steal our belongings, injure or kill us, rape our children, or that in an instant, we could lose everything we own and have to start from scratch. Most people (since they cannot imagine this or deny such things can happen) are not mentally prepared to take the necessary and appropriate actions. Their failure to do so may very well render them a victim if such an occasion arises.

A bully does not pick on someone his own size. He picks on the weak and defenseless because it gives him power. Likewise, a thief is not going to spend time trying to break into a well-protected house; that will slow him down. Instead they will seek out those that are not fortified with such things as alarms, security lights, and watch dogs.

A gang of attackers is like a group of bullies looking for the easy targets first. It is your job to make sure you are physically and mentally prepared and have a good game plan to handle the situations that come your way. So let us take a moment and address each emotional situation you must prepare for and some ways you can start to deal with them now.

1) Loss of a loved one

This is a category we need to address and is one that neither you nor I want to have to cope with, especially not during a time of disaster. But we must prepare for it. The easiest way to start handling it, and to make a plan for it, is to talk about it. First talk about it with your spouse. You might cry at the thought as you talk, but you must face the realization that it can happen. You must talk about what and how each of you will deal with it.

My husband and I have been married for over 30 years. I love him dearly and rely on his love, strength, and support in all I do. Having to think about him never being at my side again or to have to carry on without him brings me to tears as I cannot even begin to imagine it. I certainly have found it difficult to even contemplate the thought that it could happen in a disaster situation, and that I would have to take care of everything on my own with my children. That is, of course, as long as neither of them perished in the disaster event as well (as I am blessed to have a son and a daughter).

I met people and worked with people who lost their spouse and children in accidents and disasters and were forced to stand up and boldly carry on, though I am sure at that moment they would have loved to have had the world around them just stop.

Knowing the importance of mentally being prepared, my husband and I take time to talk about what we will do. I will be honest and tell you I cry every time we talk about it. My husband tells me I am the strongest person he knows. If something does happen to my husband during an event, I know I must and will follow the plan we made together. I will do what I have to do for the benefit of all the others I love in my life (children, family, etc.) and to ensure my family's survival, even if it means I must abandon his body somewhere and move on. He will do the same and so must you. I know I will take the steps necessary in such a high emotional time because I have prepared mentally to do so. I played the scenario in my brain so when my flesh is weak, my brain will help me to do what we planned. I still do not like the thought of having to do so and neither will you, but you still must prepare for it.

Don't be afraid to address this topic, and certainly do not make the fatal mistake of avoiding it. You must also address what happens if a child dies during an event, or if you have a team and one of your team member dies since most teams have designated jobs. Address death and how you will handle it and the fear of it loses its power.

Once you have a grip with the reality of death, you need to talk to your children about it. One of the greatest examples of teaching your children about death which I have ever been a witness to in my lifetime is from the "Crocodile Hunter." Because his children were around the death of animals, he and his wife helped their children understand it was all part of the cycle of life. When he died and the world mourned his death, his sweet daughter, who you could tell loved her daddy with all her heart, boldly stood before a huge crowd and gave honor to her dad and shared the love she had for him causing most to cry even harder. Did she and does she still miss her daddy? I am sure she does with all her heart. Still, he somehow taught her not to fear death and the importance of carrying on. We all must do the same thing for our children so if something does happen to us during a disaster event, not only did we teach them a game plan and how to survive, we gave them the strength to love us and let us go so they can do what they need to do to carry on. They never will forget us but we should not be the reason they become a victim either!

2) Dealing with deadly bullies -

A bully can come in all shapes and forms. If you do not defend yourself, you will become their prize. Most of us who are not around gangs, terrorist groups, etc. do not have to live with the type of reality that lifestyle brings into a person's life. For the most part, we are law abiding citizens who care about our fellow man and do not intend to harm anyone. But there are many in this world that are always looking for the right moment to build up their confidence by inflicting pain on those they believe they can hurt or control. You must understand that there are many bullies in this world who want what you have; who hate you because of your skin color; because you are a woman; because you have a different religious belief than they have; because they think you have more money than they do and that you owe it to them, etc. An evil-minded person will make up many excuses regarding why it is their right to steal, inflict bodily harm on you, or kill you. They will take without asking and kill without blinking an eye. You, however, must not set yourself up to be their victim. For most normal people, this is hard to comprehend. Understand – You cannot talk down a bully. You must think smarter, move faster, have more skills, and be willing to take action against them.

Have you ever watched the Christmas Story? In the movie, a taller boy picks on three smaller boys almost throughout the entire movie until one day, Ralphie (the main character), had enough. He loses it and starts wailing on his nemesis. In that one act of fighting back, the bully is put in his place and no longer is a problem.

The bullies we face today are much more dangerous, much more evil, and much more determined. If we are ever faced with such a situation that requires our immediate response, we must be just as determined as they are, if not more so. Notice I said immediate response, not "I will ponder or think about how I will handle it".

Determining how you will defend yourself and your loved ones, getting the appropriate training, and mentally preparing your mind to respond immediately to a threat are all vital to surviving an attack situation.

I have been a missionary for over 30 years. My goal has always been to help people, not hurt them. When we began responding to disasters and had to deal with gangs, desperate people, and mentally unstable people, I knew it was time to get prepared to defend myself if my team-members or I became prey for the evil minded in the world.

My family and I registered for a gun safety course, self-defense, and shooting and evading training. I never shot a gun before, never wanted to shoot a gun, and the thought of doing so made me sick to my stomach. I hired a retired Navy Seal to train us. Since he knew what I did for a living, he helped to train me on technique and accuracy but first he had to help me overcome the mental block I had about defending myself to the point of taking someone else's life. As I stood at the range for the very first time getting ready to shoot, and trying really hard not to throw up, he paused, took my gun, looked me in the eyes, and told me these words which I have never forgotten. He said, "Eve, in the Bible

God had his people defend themselves. You must understand there are two types of people in this world: those who are kind, loving, and who just want to live a peaceful life, and those who cannot even be considered people. You must look at them like wild animals. Their intent is simply to take, hurt, and destroy you, so it will either be you that falls at that moment in time or it will be them. Someone who wants to harm or kill you is not a person. They are animals. If you have to use your gun to protect yourself, it will not be because a kind loving person is coming at you but because a wild animal is attempting to attack you. If you hesitate you will die, and they will live another day to take someone else out." Then he put the gun back in my hand and said, "You shoot to kill any wild animal coming at you and do not hesitate! You take them out in one shot!"

Taking the wild animals out in one shot is what he taught me to do. I pray I never have to fall back on that skill, but if I do, I will not hesitate, nor should you.

There are also other forms of defensive devices you should look into as well so you have many options in your kit – things like stun guns, Tasers, knives, wasp spray, personal hand-to-hand combat skills, etc. Once you decide what and how you will defend yourself, you need to spend the money and get properly trained since your life one day may depend on it.

Like all the areas of relief I talk about, the more options you have the better chance you will have to deal with whatever situation you might face.

3) **Feeding the hungry -**

You must realize (and I know I already touched on this topic) that there will be many who are hungry and you will not be able to provide for them all. In fact, depending on how well you are prepared, you may not be able to feed any of them, not if you and your family want to survive.

Now is the time to prepare yourself mentally for how you will handle all the starving people who want food from you. They will expect you to share because they need you to want to share. They will pull at your emotions and your responsibility to be neighborly. When you do not or cannot help them, I doubt they will just walk quietly away. They will cry, plead, demand, and may even become violent. You must know how to respond or you will act out of guilty feelings that they shamefully, and wrongfully accused you of.

To me, this is most frustrating because the people who will guilt you into providing for them are the same ones who you worked with, went to church with, or your children were in sports with. They are the ones who thought you were nuts for preparing and probably even told you so. They will be the people who told you, with a laugh, that their game plan was not to prepare but to come to your house so you could care for them if anything ever happened. They continued spending their money on vacations, going out to eat, etc. instead of being responsible and setting aside the appropriate supplies they would need for their family.

What sort of friend tells you they are going to keep spending their money on luxuries and yet tells you that your supplies will be their supplies during hard times? Yet when disaster happens, so many people who worked hard, saved, and had to forego such things as vacations in order to be prepared for a disaster will try to help them because they feel guilty if they do not, and in turn, become a victim just like the rest of them.

Like I said, I have been a missionary for many years and have spent much of that time helping people in need. Yes, there are some who cannot provide for themselves and who we need to do our best to help, especially the children who are the innocent victims, but realize you will not be able to help everyone. It is a shame that there are many who choose to squander their money on toys and never prepare for the hardships or the well-being of their families, and then expect you to take care of them.

For those of us who want to help our fellow man, this is a tough topic. In a normal world, we would respond with, of course I will help those in need, but you must realize that most of the people during and after a crisis are in need. If all you have is enough to provide for your family, you will have to turn them away.

This truly is something you must determine now and stick to it. **REMEMBER! REMEMBER! REMEMBER!** - Everyone has the same opportunity you have to prepare now and if they choose not to, it is **NOT** your fault. You need to remember that by their refusal to prepare, they chose to starve and suffer. If you are able to do something to assist, then you should, but you must predetermine who that will be or you will find yourself quickly without food just like the rest of them. The only innocent are the young children or the institutionalized elderly who have no voice in getting prepared. There will be too many to help, and you will have to turn many away. Taking care of them in a short-term crisis will be much easier than a long term – several years or more.

You need to prepare your heart and mind for the agony you may see people in: crying parents pleading for food for their children, and children crying for food who may have lost their parents. Determine now your response. If you plan to assist as many as you are able, make sure to stock extra food for them. Eventually, you will need to stop unless your goal is to teach them to provide for themselves, which in the long run (if they give you the opportunity and are willing to learn) will be your best bet.

When a population of people is without food, they will do whatever they deem necessary to get some. Be prepared and respond accordingly.

Remember the Black Friday example I used before? On that one frantic shopping day of the year, people punched pregnant women in the stomach, trampled others, started all out brawls, and even shot each other – for what? – Cheaper towels, TVs, and toys!

When a crowd loses its mind, it is like a stampede of wild elephants. Eventually they stop, but it is total chaos while they are on the rampage.

4) Fear -

Fear is an emotion that attacks the mind and can render you helpless and ultimately cause you to become a victim. There have been people who were so fearful, it actually caused them to have a heart attack and die.

101

Fear is an emotion you need to work on now. It will arise in many areas of your life when disaster or chaos seems to rule the land. Fear can grip you so hard you cannot move, think, or act. It can, if allowed, be what causes the end of your existence. Or, fear can be the emotion you take control of and allow it to motivate you to become someone you never thought you could be, and a catalyst to help you achieve things you never thought you would be able to do.

Many times in our lives, fear is a made up of irrational thoughts or worries which hinders us from accomplishing what we want to do in life. Thoughts like: I do not have the skills to do that; I will fail if I try; People will think I am crazy; No one will love me; There is no way I could handle that; I am afraid to be alone, etc.

Fear is a tool that limits your ability to respond, thrive, and achieve what you thought was impossible.

Then there is true fear: someone pulls a gun on you, your child is lost or kidnapped, you lost your job and do not know how you will pay your bills, you are out of money and you have no food to feed your family, your loved one is being sent off to war, etc.

Different fears, different situations, one solution.

The one thing I can think of to help you deal with and potentially overcome your fears is to address them and learn ways to handle what is causing the fear so it no longer is a fear. Not addressing your fears allows them to take root within you and to flourish at its will, which could render you helpless and make you a victim.

I remember as a child my brother, sister, and I had to take swimming lessons. We hated it because we were afraid. One day, mom was driving us to swim class and we hid under the blanket in the back seat of the car hoping she would think we just disappeared. Our brilliant idea did not work and we found ourselves in class being forced to do something that scared us. However, we discovered that with time it wasn't as bad as we thought it would be. Eventually we all loved swimming. The fear of the water and the thought we might drown were no longer in control of our lives because we learned skills to help us swim, tread water if we should fall in, and float on our backs. These techniques and skills helped us not to be afraid. Since then, I love swimming. My parents helped us overcome a fear by teaching us a life-saving skill and so can you.

Let us look at steps you can take now to take control of any fears you or your family may have so they (the fears) will not be a negative factor in your survival plan. Some fear is healthy as it prevents you from becoming over confident and cocky, but fear to the point of immobilization is deadly.

Remember, many fears are unhealthy and just a way we protect ourselves (so we think) or way outs we give ourselves from ever trying to achieve things. Then there are fears that are healthy because they warn us of true dangers. Those dangers are ones that everyone needs solutions and a game plan to handle. Fear will run rampant in a disaster crisis so addressing the rational and irrational fears and how you will overcome and plan for them is a very important step in preparedness.

By making your preparedness plan, you should have already addressed some of the fears such as where will you meet up if a crisis occurs, where will you ultimately go, how you will survive, and you may even have addressed what to do and how to handle the bullies of the world. However, if you, let's say told your family, "If someone tries to steal our food or harm one of us, we will just take them out" but you did not teach them any skills or laid out any plans for them to follow, then all you did is give lip service. You didn't really address the actual fear they will face, and you didn't teach them how to take control of the situation.

Let's put this into perspective. If my parents had told my siblings and me that if we fell into the water, we should just swim back to shore, tread water, or float on our back but never taught us the skills we needed, chances are we probably would have drowned if we fell into the lake or a pool. Why? Because we would have panicked and not had the skills to help us survive.

As tedious as this may seem to some of the fearless or overconfident people in this world, it is a step in your preparedness plan you do not want to overlook.

Start by sitting down together as a family or team and have everyone put their fears on the table. This will be hard for some people. They will try to hide things. Your round table of conversation must be open and safe. No one should be allowed to tease another because of a fear they have. Once you know the fears that are hindering your loved ones or team members, you address them and come up with steps to overcome or work with those fears.

Sometimes however, our best laid plans for helping someone overcome a fear can backfire and you will have to find another way to help them.

I was terrified of snakes. I knew they could bite and I wanted no part of being outside or being where they might be. This was rather impossible though because we spent much of our time in the Great North Woods. My dad was going to show me and my sisters, who also were afraid of snakes, that there was nothing to fear. He picked up a garden snake and basically said, "See it won't hurt you" and then it bit him! Yes, we all took off running and screaming and my dad was, still to this day, really mad at that snake. We all laugh about it now, but back then it only increased our fears. So my dad had to take a different approach and taught us how to watch out for them and how to avoid them. He did not give up just because his first idea failed; he simply had to find a new way to help us. Did our fear of snakes go away? No, but we were no longer afraid to go outdoors because we used the steps he had shown us to avoid them. Today I spend much of my time in the wilderness where many venomous snakes live. I still do not like snakes, especially those that bite, but I do not let the thought of them hinder me from living a life I enjoy. The lesson to learn from this is – if at first you do not succeed, keep trying until you do!

Once you address the hidden fears, start to address the serious and potential fears of true dangers, and then come up with detailed (not lip service) plans on how you will handle them. Get the training you need from skilled, trained professionals and build up the confidence and "know how" of your family, so when a dangerous situation arises, you, your family, and your team will not be victims of those attempting to inflict fear on you. Instead, learn how to handle the situations and turn the tables on the bullies of the world, or even on Mother Nature. You may not be able to stop a hurricane but you sure can know what to do if one is heading your way! You may not be able to prevent an evil minded band of thugs from stealing all you have but you can, when they start heading for your house, learn how to send them running in the opposite direction.

Remember my example of Ralphie and the Christmas Story? When Ralphie finally had enough and pummeled the neighborhood bully who was terrorizing him and his buddies, the big bad bully no longer was a threat. He was reduced to nothing but a joke among the school children and none of them feared him anymore.

Fear of the unknown, fear of things changing for the worse, fear of being alone, and fear of being shot at or attacked, etc. can and should be addressed and dealt with. It will make each person stronger and your family or team more secure and effective. It is true that you are only as strong as your weakest link so strengthen all the weak links. Every time you strengthen a link, you become more empowered and your outcome in a disaster area and your survival increases.

Now you might be saying at this point, heck, I am just trying to prepare in the event of a tornado or a flood. My response to you is that even in those situations, my team and I have seen people rendered helpless by fear. Fear of bugs, fear of sleeping outside, fear of being looted, shot or raped, fear of what the future holds, fear of having to go potty outside, fear of having to survive a few days without electricity, fear of getting their hands dirty, fear of germs, etc. The list of fears we have seen in a disaster area is huge. Some are real, some annoying, and many unrealistic. If that is what we have seen first-hand in events where the whole country has not been affected, imagine what it would be like in a catastrophic event.

Fear is fear. It does not matter the size of the event. Large or small, it is still something you should and really need to address. Trying to address it after an event happens is the same as saying you will deal with it when the time comes, but when a disaster strikes it is too late.

If you really want to be prepared, you will not overlook this important step in your preparation plans!

5) Observation -

I know I have mentioned this before but it deserves repeating. If you want to survive and thrive you must hone and practice your skills of observation. Most people are simply not observant.

You must take the time to become aware of your surroundings and the behavior of others. It is all part of being mentally prepared, so practice it.

6) Letting Go -

Yes, you may have to let go of someone you love, but that is not what I want to address here since I previously addressed that topic. What I want to talk about is preparing your mind to let go of your old life, your life of comfort and conveniences as well as your safety and security that has always been provided, for the most part, by others. Letting go of the life you love and enjoy and preparing your mind for the potential of being thrown into a life where there are no more restaurants for you to go to, no toilets for you to use, no showers, no clean clothes, no air-conditioning, no security, cell phones, computers, theaters, TVs, or radios. The question to ask yourself is – Are you ready for a life of no comforts? Are you mentally prepared to lose everything you own and have to start all over again? My guess is probably not.

We all, for the most part, have lived a very comfortable life, some more than others. But for most, even the poor in our country, have or have access to such luxuries as a place to stay, bathroom facilities, medical care, cell phone service, computers, food, etc. In the blink of an eye though, you may find all those modern conveniences and creature comforts we all take for granted and enjoy gone. The question you must ask yourself is how will you handle it mentally?

It is not uncommon for us to see totally dysfunctional and distraught people in a disaster area because their once beautiful life has been unmercifully ripped away from them and completely destroyed. Many rise to the occasion and are grateful to be alive while others are debilitated by it and become useless.

On one major event we responded to, I saw a man sitting on a small stump of a tree that was destroyed. He was texting on his phone. I was shocked because we did not have any cell service but he was texting. Understand everything was destroyed and his family was sitting off in the grass just crying but he was texting. When I walked up to the man and asked him what he was doing, it took some time to get his attention and to get him to acknowledge me. When I again inquired about what he was doing, he said he was texting everyone he knew. I asked him if I could use his phone to get his family some assistance and he reluctantly handed it to me. When I informed him his phone was dead and he had no service for texting, he said he knew but he had to text people anyway. When I told him his family needed him and were waiting for him, his response was, "I need to text. Will you go help them?" I was surprised and realized this man was so traumatized and overwhelmed; he was totally incapable of helping his wife or crying children. We stepped in and helped his family and he proceeded to stand up and take off down the road texting. Once his family was taken care of we located our missing "texter" and returned him to his family and worked to bring him back around to reality.

Our "texter" was an important, respected individual in the world of business. He was very successful in his job and was used to giving directions and having others do the work. They lived a very comfortable life and never had to worry about not having. He always expected his life to be the same – wonderful. The disaster, however, completely changed that and took away his self-confidence and ability to function which rendered him useless and caused him to abandon his family in their hour of need. This man is someone who really had no excuse not to be prepared and yet he had no supplies, no game plan, no skills, nothing!

His story is only one of many that we have seen like that and yet we have also seen and worked with other individuals and communities that prepared scenarios so that when the time came and they were faced with the unthinkable, they became a part of the solution and not part of the problem. They took control of their situation, helped their fellow man, and worked hard to regain the way of life they lost. They understood it was going to take time but with hard work, encouragement, and a desire to make it happen, they accomplished what many believed would be impossible. They never lost their love of country, love of one another, their moral character, or their desire to live. They had a common goal and worked together to achieve it.

How you handle the loss of everything is up to you. Just remember this. When disaster strikes, there are no do overs, no turning back the hands of time, and no second chances.

I have seen great acts of heroism and cowardice; I have seen beautiful acts of love and compassion, and terrible acts of hatred and evil. I have seen times of tremendous unity and times of unbelievable chaos. I have had the privilege to help and assist those who lost it all but were thankful for the helping hand and worked very hard to overcome the hurdles and obstacles before them. Unfortunately, I also dealt with those who do not even deserve to be mentioned in this book except to tell you they lacked any compassion or humanity and their only desire was to prey on anyone and everyone they could.

What type of person do you plan to be? When a crisis hits, whatever remains of your past existence will be what it will be and you cannot undo it, but you can work to rebuild it. So, if you want to be strong for all those around you and have the best outcome as possible, start mentally preparing for it now and help all your family members do the same.

Chapter 14

Question 11

Are You Ready for an Epidemic?

Most people, when preparing for a disaster, do not think about epidemics but instead think about broken bones and wounds.

I know I touched briefly on this in the medical section, but now I want to talk about some of the diseases I mentioned in that section. So once again, I must state that I am not diagnosing, prescribing, or telling you how to treat a disease. I am merely sharing information about what the different diseases are and how others have chosen to handle them in order to get you researching things out yourself.

So let's look at some of the illnesses that could take place if a long-term disaster event occurred.

RABIES

Today, for the most part, few people have to worry about rabies. Though we are told and understand that bats and raccoons may carry the virus, it is not a big concern for most. After a disaster, when more animals are on the loose and dogs and other animals have not received rabies vaccinations, it could become more prevalent so you should familiarize yourself with its symptoms or keep it for a reference in your emergency kit. Symptoms of a rabid animal:

- Animals may or may not appear sick, bewildered, or vicious. The phrase "mad dog" actually originated from the behavior of a rabid animal. What most people do not realize is that a rabid animal may also act normal, overly friendly, or extremely docile. Because of this, it may be difficult to know if an animal actually is rabid or not. One action that should alert you to the possibility that an animal is rabid is when a normally aggressive or standoffish animal is acting friendly or has changed its behavior such as a bat flying outside at noontime.

- When more animals start contracting the rabies virus, it is likely more humans will come in contact with this disease so it is important to know how it affects people.

Symptoms in humans

- The incubation period for people has a very wide range, anywhere from less than 10 days to several years though for most it is supposedly between 30-60 days.
- Usual first symptoms are pain, tingling, or itching shooting from the bite site.
- Other symptoms are flu like: fevers, chills, fatigue, muscle aches, and irritability. The only thing that is different than basic flu symptoms is the abnormal pain at the site of the bite.
- Eventually other symptoms are: high fever, confusion, irritability, seizures, and comas.
- A unique condition may also develop called hydrophobia or aerophobia which is contraction or spasms of the breathing muscles when they are exposed to water or when air is puffed at them.

Knowing that rabies may one day become a potential problem, I like to make people aware that it is something they should think about and find solutions for. Most people believe that the only solution is a series of rabies shots. If those shots are not available, what will you do? Remember the die or try mentality. Native Americans, naturalists, herbalists, and even homeopaths have come up with ideas and solutions on how to handle this and other illnesses. Do I know for certain if their ideas will work – no, but it does warrant looking into if you want to have a game plan because no medical kit on the market contains rabies shots.

CHOLERA

Cholera is no longer common in the United States because of our modern sewage system and water treatment plants, but it was prevalent in the early 1800's.

You contract cholera by consuming food or water that is contaminated with a bacterium called vibrio cholera. The water is contaminated by human feces that contain the infection. Cholera is an infection that affects the small intestine. The symptoms can be profuse watery diarrhea accompanied with vomiting and muscle cramps. Due to the severity of the diarrhea, it can lead to severe dehydration or death if the dehydration isn't controlled. It is also important to know that there may not be any symptoms at all for some individuals. Incubation time is anywhere from a few hours to approximately 5 days after ingestion of the bacteria.

Because this disease is common where there is war, famine, over-crowding, and poor sanitation, it is easy to see how it could be a problem that could present itself if a major disaster occurred and our sanitation plants are not in working order.

DEHYDRATION

Dehydration is common after a disaster because people eat old food causing them to get food poisoning, contracted an illness causing them to lose bodily fluids, or heat exhaustion from working long hours in the sun doing clean up with little water consumption. It is important to avoid this by taking simple measures such as drinking as much liquids (not alcohol) as possible and having electrolytes in your kit for when you are in need.

Symptoms consist of rapid heart rate, low blood pressure causing a person to feel as if they may faint, dry mucous membranes, and loss of skin elasticity. Dehydration, when not treated, can lead to shock and death in just hours.

Know the signs and symptoms and work to avoid this condition. Pay attention to your family and team-members as well.

When we are working in the field, we have a rule on water breaks – you never skip them! Depending on the heat, our scheduled breaks may be as frequent as every 15 minutes. It does not mean we stop working and take a sit down break. It implies that every 15 minutes we pause, drink, and then keep on working until the next water break.

TYPHOID FEVER

Typhoid fever, just like cholera, is contracted by drinking water or eating food that is contaminated with sewage that contains bacteria, or has been handled by someone infected with a bacteria called "Salmonella typhi." Unlike Cholera that affects the small intestine, typhoid fever results when the bacteria is ingested and is then spread through the bloodstream causing havoc.

Typical symptoms are:

Constant fever that may go as high as 104 degrees and last for several weeks. Historically, improvement usually begins around week 3 of the illness for those not treated with antibiotics.

Other symptoms include:

- Diarrhea
- Extreme fatigue
- Body aches, including headaches
- Poor appetite
- Pneumonia

The incubation period is 1-2 weeks which makes it difficult as many people in that time period could consume the contaminated food and water before the first symptom appears. If many are drinking from the same water source, you could potentially have a serious epidemic.

A few of the issues with this illness are 1) It is not uncommon for a person to have a relapse; 2) Some people may become carriers of the disease; and 3) For some, it can become a chronic infection.

Prior to the use of antibiotics, it is stated that the mortality rate with this infection was 20% but with the use of antibiotics the rate dropped to only 1-2%. It is also noteworthy to mention that those using an antibiotic had a higher chance for relapse but the duration of the illness was also greatly reduced from 3-4 weeks down to 7-

10 days. The cause of death usually occurred from intestinal bleeding, other intestinal issues, and pneumonia.

TYPHUS

Many people think that typhus and Typhoid Fever are the same infection but they are not. Typhus is the result of a bacterium called Rickettsia. There are two forms of typhus. (All the scientific information on the difference of the two forms is not important for your understanding of what it will do to you, but if you would like to get detailed information, as I am simply giving the basics, look up Rickettsia typhi and Rickettsia prowazekki.)

The milder form of typhus, also referred to as "jail fever" or murine typhus, is actually called endemic typhus. The second less common but most dangerous form of typhus is called epidemic typhus. A person can have a relapse with Typhus just like they can with Typhoid Fever.

Unlike Cholera or Typhoid Fever, both types of typhus are carried by different animals such as mice, rats, etc. and transmitted to humans by lice, ticks, or even fleas. "Jail Fever" usually results in poor hygiene areas that are over-crowded and in less sanitary areas such as refugee camps, homeless shelters, and unclean jails.

However, epidemic typhus is transmitted through lice and ticks. Their host is either the flying squirrels or human beings. That is correct; the most dangerous form of typhus can be transmitted through human body lice! Past history shows that for those who fell victim to this form of typhus and who went untreated had a 10-60% mortality rate. ("Jail Fever" had a much lower mortality rate of only approximately 2 %.)

As you can see, though epidemic typhus is less common in our current world, it is the more deadly and could become an issue if hygiene, or lack thereof, is neglected.

Symptoms of "Jail Fever" or endemic typhus are:

- Fever that can go as high as 106 degrees Fahrenheit and last up to 2 weeks
- Joint, muscle, and abdominal pain
- Headache
- Dull red rash that starts in the central part of the body and then spreads
- Nausea
- Vomiting
- Dry cough

Symptoms of Epidemic typhus include:

- Flu like symptoms: severe headaches, joint, and muscle pain, chills, cough
- Red rash begins on chest and spreads over entire body
- Fever of 104 degrees Fahrenheit
- Confusion
- Low blood pressure
- In severe cases, some people may develop areas of bleeding in the skin.

If there is an outbreak of this infection, it is important to get rid of the lice. Lice will die when they have to go at least 5 days without blood to consume. Therefore, remove all clothing with lice and boil but do not reuse for at least 5 days. My recommendation would be to err on the side of caution and if you are able to do without those articles of clothing, burn them. Bathing is a must, and there are natural alternative options and insecticides that will also help so consider learning about them.

When disaster happens, it is important to have some idea of different types of illnesses and infections so you can work to avoid or reduce your risk of catching them. Knowledge of your water source will be vital, as will avoiding high populated, unsanitary, areas.

Once again, I am not allowed to give medical advice (due to the fact I am not a doctor) on how to handle these illnesses, but I am able to give you some thoughts to ponder. If these illnesses are transmitted from bacteria in the water, food, or even body lice, what can you do to purify or protect your sources? Just like during flu season, is there something you could do to boost your immune system to protect yourself? Are there alternative options you could search out and use in the event anyone came down with any of these illnesses?

It is your choice to decide if you will research these questions or not. Just realize that if no medical care is available, you will need to handle whatever comes along. Having an understanding of these illnesses and others such as smallpox, influenza, chickenpox, malaria, Rocky Mountain spotted fever, etc. will be very beneficial for you. Have a game plan on what you will do if such outbreaks occur and don't believe the lie that there is nothing you can do. There are answers and possibilities worth looking into. I may not be allowed to give them to you in this book but you do have the right to search for them.

Since you most likely will not remember all the diseases and their symptoms, I recommend you compile a folder with information on each one for future reference if a disaster happens.

Collect and add to your medical kit whatever tools of assistance you come up with as you think about the questions I gave you. Do not rely on anyone else for the answers – you find them!

Chapter 15

Question 12

Are You Ready To Barter?

Are you the type of person who loves to wheel and deal at rummage sales and car dealerships, or are you the type of person who merely walks into a department store, pays the full price, and leaves?

Are you the type of person who avoids, like the plague, any and all garage sales, farmers markets, and flea markets? Do you hate or are you afraid to haggle over the price of something?

If you avoid going to rummage sales and the like, I recommend you start frequenting them so you can learn the art of bartering.

Bartering is a skill you will need. It is not about just going to a friend and saying, "Hey, how about I give you a pair of jeans for your loaf of bread?" It is about learning to communicate, determine fair value so you do not get taken advantage of, and about relatively equal exchange. If you refuse to go to flea markets now, imagine your culture shock when you actually need to begin swapping your unnecessary items for necessary ones! People will walk all over you and take advantage of you because they will see you as an easy target coming from a mile away.

When I go to yard sales, I watch those around me closely. I can easily pick out those who will pay top dollar for an item and those who will work to get the same item reduced down to pocket change. To be a successful rummager, it takes a little knowledge and a lot of boldness. Please do not mistake boldness for rudeness. I will give you an example of both.

BOLDNESS - One day my son and I went rummaging and found an item we needed, but this item in a regular store was expensive. Since it was in good condition at a yard sale, we anticipated a high price. We checked the item over but there was no sales sticker on it. My son asked the person how much he wanted for it and the person responded, "Make me an offer." I told the man I hated when people did that because I had no idea what he was thinking he wanted for it and it gave us no place to start negotiating. He came back with, "Well, just make me an offer." I was ready to walk away but my son boldly looked at this man and said, "OK, since you will not give us a price, I will make you an offer – how about $1.00?" The man was shocked because the price was way under the value. He in turned came back with, "Are you kidding me, it is an expensive item." My son responded, "Yes it is, and we asked you what you wanted for it but you did not know and insisted we give you a price. I picked a price as you stated I must. It is now your option to accept or deny it, but if you deny it, put a price on it so people will know what you want next time." The man looked at my son and said, "You got me there and you are right, OK, it is yours for $1.00!" That man could have rejected my son's offer, which we thought he would, but he realized my son had a good point. They were too lazy to price any of their items and were throwing the work of pricing onto their customers. He rewarded my son and his boldness by giving him the item we wanted at the price my son offered.

RUDENESS –A woman notoriously known for her rudeness came to a rummage sale I was holding. She went around our sale area and gathered up priced items totaling over $50.00 and then told me she would only pay 20 cents for it all. Seriously?! Did she really think I would accept her offer? Worse yet, she started arguing with me and attempted to walk off with everything after she plopped down the 20 cents. This woman had a used items store and was always trying to get everything for nothing. We stopped the woman and demanded she either pay the price or hand it over. I would have reduced the price to a lower amount if she would have made a fair offer for the items but her behavior and ridiculous offer made me refuse her the sale at all.

You will not do well in the world of bartering if you cheat, steal, and scream your way through it. You will get a bad reputation, as this woman has, and no one will want to deal with you.

During times of disaster, the things you consider valuable now will be deemed junk, and the items you see as junk now may be your most valuable item.

When thinking about bartering, if the occasion should arise as it has in other countries experiencing food shortages and other hardships, you need to think on a level of essentials, not so much luxuries. Will some people barter for luxuries? Yes, but understand that luxury may be something like toilet paper or feminine hygiene items, not sofas and high-end jewelry.

When you prepare for a disaster, think of essential items such as extra food, water filters, medical supplies, shoes, socks, fuel sources, liquor, seeds, bullets, etc. Have extra of these items on hand so that if you run short on something and need to make a trade with someone, you will have something they most likely need or could use. Not having barter supplies means that if you run short on something, you will have to take from your items you are currently using to get something you deem more important at the time, or do without.

Skills are also an important bartering tool. If you have essential skills that can help or better life in some way, then you can barter that skill for what you need. Just make sure to get payment up front when you show up to work. Do not make a potential error and agree to get paid later, as later most likely will never happen.

I have been in disaster areas where bartering was a common every day event as people were trying to survive. Sometimes it was done peacefully. Sometimes fighting broke out. Always be fair or it can come back to bite you in the world of bartering. Also, do not just give things away at the beginning because if you do, people will expect you to continue that pattern for them.

I want you to remember the story of Joseph in the Bible. God had Joseph prepare for a famine that was going to affect the land. For 7 years he stored up and when the famine hit and people ran out of food, he opened the store house. BUT, people did not get the food for free. They first paid with money, and then their livestock, their land, and finally themselves. It is not being greedy. Once again, nearly everyone has the same opportunity to prepare as you do except for the children and institutionalized elderly. Putting a reasonable price on what you worked hard for is not unfair or thoughtless. It is justified and reasonable.

So think about what you would want to have on hand to barter, and start practicing this skill; you will be grateful you did. It is fun now, but during a crisis it will be critical.

Chapter 16

Question 13

What Skills Do You Have?

Here is reality as I have seen it in a disaster area. Those with beneficial and essential skills do much better than those who have none.

When you have a skill that others need, they are more likely to take care of you and protect you. If you had a doctor who wanted to join your group of survivors, would you not welcome them with open arms? Of course you would because your thought would be, "If someone is injured or gets sick, we will have someone to help us." You will make sure that doctor eats, has clothing, and protection because you deem them essential to your survival. On the other hand, if someone came in requesting to be part of your group and you asked them what skills they have and they reply "nothing," how likely will you let them join? You will see them as someone who will just take up space and eat all your food.

If you do not have a skill that would be needed after a disaster event or long term survival event, then learn one or several *NOW*. You are truly never too old to learn. Start learning how to properly can food, sew clothing, repair cars, working with wood, animal care, gardening, alternative health care, hunting, etc. All these skills give you value and open a door for your potential acceptance into a survival group if you ever desire or need to join one. Gaining and learning new skills is something you seriously need to consider and get started on. Do *NOT* wait for tomorrow because tomorrow never seems to get here. There is always something else you want to do.

Some people plan on weathering an event by themselves. This is really not advisable since you cannot do everything on your own, and there is increased safety in numbers. There are those unique individuals though who may be able to survive by themselves, but they have had many years of training, which usually started when they were a child and were interested in living in the great outdoors. This is the exception, not the norm. So if surviving on your own has not been a way of life for you, it should not become your choice during a disaster because you most likely do not have the skills, and will eventually become a victim.

You have the ability to make yourself valuable by learning one or more essential skills. You may be a hard worker, but no one will know that until you are given the chance to prove yourself which you may only get when you bring something of worth to the table – so start learning!

Chapter 17

Question 14

What Is Your Team's Game Plan?

I am addressing this question because at events and in private consultations, I hear time and time again some really terrible plans that can be costly in all areas of your survival or even in the formation of a team.

Frequent issues people are facing with their potential team:

- They gather every week for a meeting and talk about what they should do but after 6 or more months, nothing has been agreed or accomplished.
- The leader of the group treats everyone with rudeness and disrespect, especially the women.
- The team has no supplies except guns and bullets, and were told they do not need to worry about anything else.
- Everyone on their team is old and unable to do any physical labor.
- Everyone can gather whatever supplies they want and they will all share.
- No one on their team has skills or only skills that rely on modern, powered conveniences such as microwaves, powered tools, or ready-made/kit products.
- Their team does not believe they need to worry about defense; they will negotiate with anyone and show kindness to all.

Let's address some of these issues and set you on a path for a responsible and realistic team.

A team made up of only elderly with you being the only one with the ability to do all the work is unrealistic and will quickly fail. One person cannot do all the labor for an entire community team. (If they could, they would be the exception I spoke about previously and not need the rest of the team.) It is important to take care of the elderly, but you need to form a team with a wide range of skills, ages, and physical abilities. Many older people know how to cook, can food, wash clothing, watch the children so others can work, etc. and can play an important role in your survival team. During Katrina, we had people in assisted living homes putting together small food packages and assisting in our staging area where we packaged all the relief supplies. We had one older woman in a wheel chair putting plastic ware into sealed bags. Older people have great value in all areas of life. Include them as part of your team since many will bring great wisdom to the table that will help you out greatly. You will need the young as well as the old to make up your team.

You will also need people with a wide range of skills. If your team believes they do not have any valuable or useful skills, start appointing people to learn different skills and then teach each other so if something happens to one person, there are still others on your team who know how to do the tasks. Skills are vital to the success of any group or team.

To form a team where you are told you will need nothing but guns and bullets implies their intensions are to take from others what they need. They will be the bullies I talked about earlier in this book. They are filled with hate and lack any sort of moral character. I advise you to run from that team and find another. Inform the new team that an irresponsible, low-life group has formed so you can be prepared for them.

If you joined a group where the team leader is rude and insulting to women and he makes you uncomfortable, find or form a new group. It is highly likely that this behavior will magnify under stress, more rapidly deteriorating good order and cooperation. A team should work together, encourage each other, and build each other up, not tear each other down. You have the option to leave before your survival depends on it. Take it.

A huge problem and the most frequent complaint I found among the people who seek me out for consultation is that they meet and meet and meet yet never form a game plan. They simply just keep talking and nothing is ever accomplished. Their fallback plan becomes "everybody will just pool all their supplies and share" – this is terrible on all accounts!

If you cannot accomplish anything now when things are normal, how are you ever going to accomplish anything during a time of crisis and chaos? A group like this tells me that they do not have a game plan and figure if they just keep on talking, one will magically appear! Unfortunately, the person that organized the group obviously did not have a plan, and is certainly not a leader. Other than getting people together for a social gathering, their lack of knowledge, focus, determination, and skills does not allow them to guide the group into creating a well laid out game plan if they should need it, nor to implement such a plan. They obviously know they need to form a group but have no vision or direction on how to go about putting an effective one together. If in time of peace they cannot form a plan, what happens when an emergency occurs? They will possibly just talk everyone to death! Seriously, if in 6 months after meeting once per week, you have not established a plan, it is time to close up shop and look for a new group! Your chance of thriving with a group like that is slim at best.

In a disaster area, you have to make split second decisions and the decisions you make can determine if you live or die. When I take a team into a disaster area or have to send some in alone, I do it knowing their life is my responsibility. I make sure to do everything I can to ensure they will come back home safely. I tell my relief teams that "They will be looking into the eyes of despair and those victims must be looking into the eyes of hope." I also let them know that the moment I look into their eyes and I see despair, they will be removed from the field for R&R and will not go back in until it is determined they are ready.

If a leader proves untrustworthy, they are removed from the team. If people violate the rules, they are sometimes warned (depending on the offense), and then kicked out. Each team member relies on the other and if one falls or fails, it affects us as a whole. Those that come to volunteer during a disaster have to read and agree to a code of ethics; to violate it means expulsion from the staging area or the relief teams. We have a detailed plan and it is to be adhered to. I let people know it has been tried and proven effective. When individuals came forward and volunteered, felt they could do it better, and without permission changed things, they saw the results and the delay it created in our having to undo what they did. They were removed and informed they were not welcome back. When individuals did not, or do not follow orders after being instructed regarding why things are done a specific way, they are asked to leave. When we are in an event and someone does not follow directions, they are removed from the disaster site as untrustworthy, reckless, and a danger to themselves and others. For those who refuse to leave, they are escorted out. Belittling, backstabbing, discouraging, or disparaging other team members is not tolerated.

The following is a portion of our code of ethics and rules for any volunteer coming to work for us. Though it is for our non-profit response team, it can be used to get you thinking on the code and rules by which you want your team to live or operate. You set the tone for your group. Put some thought into it now so everyone will be on the same page.

As stated, this is just a portion of our non-profit {Caring Hearts, Inc. (CHI)} code of ethics for all our relief teams:

"We will encourage not discourage, we will stand for truth not hypocrisy, we will show love not hate, our words will be of a pure heart not a corrupt one, we will be responsible, flexible, self-disciplined, and work with a quiet perseverance..."

A portion of our rules for the CHI response volunteers:

- You will follow all directions given – this is for your safety, the safety of those around you, and to ensure proper preparations of relief supplies that you are working with.

- At no time will you change the way a line is run or a packing procedure is done – these procedures have been set up for the benefit of those on the delivery side of the relief effort. We work harder here at the prep site so their job will be easier in the disaster site.
- There will be no swearing, dumb blond, racial, or dirty jokes.
- "Shortie shorts" and other improper clothing attire is not allowed - it can become a distraction to others around you.
- You will take no action to willing endanger the life of another team member.
- No team is greater than the other, it takes all of us to accomplish the mission.

Sample of the Actions that we have mandated will result in immediate removal of a volunteer:

- Aggressive or threatening behavior towards leaders or other volunteers
- Sexual misconduct or harassment
- Illegal drug use
- Refusal to follow directions

These types of behavior will not be tolerated at all. If such behavior is occurring and you feel threatened at all, immediately get assistance; do not try to handle it on your own.

I love and respect my team and they love and respect me right back. They know I mean what I say and say what I mean. They will also tell you (as I have heard them say it numerous times) "She appears like a sweet redheaded lady (which I am) but watch out if you endanger the team or the ones she loves." Reckless, thoughtless behavior is not acceptable and neither is someone unwilling to work. I truly do believe and enforce that if someone capable of working does not work, then they will not eat. Unacceptable situations will be immediately handled in a manner appropriate to the offense. My team will tell you I am not a dictator or a mean boss, I am just someone who has been placed in a position of great responsibility and I take it very seriously. My team knows I constantly have their backs (and they have mine) and am continually thinking of ways to make things better. They are my priority. I will not rest until I know they are all safe and that I have done my job to the best of my ability.

Our team is made up of mutual love and respect for each other. Each person is assigned their tasks, and we all go about handling them in the way that is best for everyone. We work together as a family because we have become a family.

Another issue that must be addressed is teams that do not believe they will ever have to defend themselves. They believe all people are good, just sometimes misunderstood. They believe that if they just show kindness to others, those same others in turn will show kindness back. However, this is not true, and there are way too many examples to prove it. Do you really believe a terrorist group will sit down and just have a cup of tea with you so that you can talk and help them understand you mean them no harm? Do you think a gang of bullies who want your possessions will just knock on your door and ask permission to rob you? There are some that have such evil built up in their heart they will never listen to reason, and could care less about what you have to say. Some will not even give you a second to speak before they act.

Defense is necessary. To form a team with no plan on how to defend yourself if you find yourself under attack leaves you vulnerable. If a group finds out you have no defense, they surely will be heading your way, considering you a no-risk source of re-supply for themselves. If after watching the news time and time again, you still believe you can talk the intruder or enemy down, I truly wish you the best of luck, and wish you well as you stand firmly (as long as you are able) in your desire to only show kindness to those who intend you harm. I pray it goes well for you.

If you are on a team where simple decisions cannot be made in 6 months, then I would not count on them to be able to do it in a time of high stress or ever. A team incapable of formulating guidelines and organizing realistic effective game plans, not able to work together as one, lacking in mutual respect and concern for all team members, or refusing to learn skills or do work is not a team you even want to consider being a part of. It is a team that is so unjustifiably arrogant and cocky that they refuse to listen to the truth, or they fail to investigate the facts in order to help save team members' lives. Either way, a no-win situation for their members.

Being part of a team can make a difference on how you survive a long-term disaster event (though also beneficial in short term events as well). It is an important decision. Many teams will interview new recruits to see if they will be a good add-on to their group. Make sure that while they are checking you out that you are checking them out as well. Do not be so desperate to find a group that you take the first one that opens the doors to you. They may decide they want you to join, but you need to make sure they meet your requirements as well. Remember Chapters 15 and 16; are you both bringing value to the table?

It is amazing to me when I hear some of the things groups of people are planning. Many have well thought out plans and should do fine. Others are so unrealistic it leaves me shaking my head in disgust or disbelief. You already know what I think about those who will prey on others and take what they want by force, but I met another group (I am sure there are more like them) that told me their game plan was to take over their local zoo and kill anyone who tried to enter it since all the animals in the zoo would become their food. They were so sincere about their belief that this plan was good and acceptable; there was no persuading them otherwise. Some days, I ask myself and those around me, "Whatever happened to common sense?"

SETTING UP A TEAM

Setting up a team is basically the same thing as setting up your own personal family game plan with a few variations, most importantly on a larger scale.

- Gather with those of like-mindedness and those you know you can trust. Then start hammering out your plan.

- Set your goals, rules, and guidelines. One important rule you must consider establishing: If you do not work, you do not eat! Some people are just lazy so have a plan in place to handle that problem right from the start.

- Make your game plan: meet up, evacuation plan, a location you will bugout to as a team if necessary, etc.

- Evaluate what skill sets you all have (write them down. Science proves that the simple act of writing things down greatly improves the chances of follow-through.)

- Determine what skill sets are still needed and either find people with those skills to join you or appoint people to learn them.

- Set training times to learn skills others have so there is more than just one person with that skill. In the disaster area, our saying is "One is none." If you have only one of an item and it breaks, you are left with nothing and so we recommend multiples of essential items. The same holds true for skills. If you have only one person who knows an important skill and they die or leave, you are left with no one to cover that area of need.

- Look at your kit needs. Every team member should have the same required items. Set the items you want each individual to bring to the table, and then verify they have gathered those supplies. For bigger items, determine how, who, and when they will be acquired.

- Your food plan should not be something like "just bring all you have and we will share." (Many made this their plan and trust me when I say; this is a terrible plan and will create many types of hardships for you.) You should have at least a 4-month food list and everyone must purchase the entire list of food. (See Chapter 6 for a suggested food list.) Doing it this way, everyone will bring the same amount of food and there should be no cause for fighting down the road. Also, plan for extras; after an event people will come forth who are not in your group who will want to join, someone's grandma, neighbor, etc. First determine beforehand if you will allow new entries. If your answer is yes, you will accept new people after a crisis, then purchase enough food to cover them; otherwise, you are stealing food from those who planned, and giving it to those who did not. This action will cause division in the group.

- Each meeting should show progress towards your ultimate goal. If you have someone who continuously shows up having accomplished nothing since the last meeting, give them warning, if the situation does not improve, you need to ask them to leave.

- Train and get training from experts, and continually work to grow your friendships and team unity. Do not allow "cliques"; they can quickly destroy the morale and unity of your group!

With time, dedication, focus, teamwork, and a well thought out plan, your team can do well if a major crisis erupts. Just please remember to always work together and do not forget the difference between right and wrong. During disasters, some people throw their humanity and morals out the window and become the "problem" in their surrounding society forgetting that one day there will be a day of reckoning and they will pay for all they did, one way or another.

Chapter 18

Question 15

Will You Have Water?

I am not going to spend a lot of time on this question as I have talked about it in Preparation Made Simple and other articles you can read. But I will say this: You need a good filter system you know works (I and all my team uses the Berkey Filter) and make sure to have back-up units and filters.

Make sure to have a water source (several if possible) that is protected since you now know some of the diseases that come from contaminated water (thus the importance of a good filter). Have a system for catching rain water. Know how to purify and distill water. Have options! Again, "One is none!" Water is a life essential requirement so you better have a plan in place on how you will get some, and how you will keep it safe and consumable. Water should be a top priority, not an after-thought!

Chapter 19

Question 16

Do You Know the Skills of Your Great-Grandparents?

Most people do not even know how to cook in this day and age, much less know the skills our great-grandparents knew.

We are so used to going to the store to buy all our food, hygiene products, laundry detergent, etc. We know how to throw the dirty laundry into the machine to wash and then dry, how to take our car to the shop for repairs, and how to push a lawn mower (though many now just pay someone else to do that job). But what if, in an instant, you found yourself having to catch or grow and prepare your food all on your own; you had to make your own detergent and had to hand wash your clothing; you had to fix your own car or go without one; or you had to be your own doctor. Could you do it? Could you hand sew your own clothes, grow your own food, hunt, fish, etc.?

Our great-grandparents did not have all the modern conveniences we have today which in turn has caused us to stop learning all the basic skills in life, and we became lazy. Back then, they worked hard, really hard, but they knew how to survive.

If a long-term disaster occurs, you will need to know those basic skills. There are classes all over this country and older people who know how to do them that would be willing to teach you – so learn now.

Understand all of them are a skill. Just take a look at gardening for example. I had people tell me that when an event happens, they will just plant some seeds and they will be fine, but they have never done it before. They do not know what type of soil they have, and do not have the knowledge to improve it if needed. They have some old seed packets they bought from the store but do not realize they will no longer grow. They do not know the difference between heirloom seeds and the cheap ones you can buy at the market. They do not know how to harvest and save seeds either. If your life depends on what you can grow in your garden, then you better make sure you can make it grow.

Gardening, both vegetables and herbs, car repair, canning food, making your own candles and soap, sewing clothes, hunting, etc. are all skills you need and want to have if you are going to be successful after a crisis where a return to "normal" may be years away, if ever. Mastering these skills also gives you significant value to others (groups or teams) since many will not know how to do them.

A time to learn a new skill is not when you need it, it is beforehand when you have the time to practice and hone your new talent.

Chapter 20

Question 17

Is Defense and Protection Really Necessary?

Having been in disaster areas, my answer would be **ABSOLUTELY**.

I know I addressed defense in other areas of this book, but it really is important and I feel the need to address it once again.

When I am doing my training classes, I take a moment and talk directly to the women and older people and let them know they easily could become a target of all the bullies/gangs on the loose looking to create more chaos than that which already exists. It is a time, in their eyes, to have some fun, but their fun is evil, corrupt, and at times ruthless. (Think of the child in school who found it funny to pull the wings off flies just because they could. The defenseless will become the 'fly' in their eyes!) If you are older, physically handicapped or a woman, my advice would be to get expert training so you can defend yourself and you will not have to rely on anyone else to protect you. You become the "fighting machine." Lord willing, you will never have to use it but if you do, you will at least have a fighting chance.

Chapter 21

Question 18

Should We Stay Put or Should We Leave?

As you start to enter the world of preparedness and begin to read magazines or listen to others who are preparing, you will hear the phrase, "bug in or bug out." It simply means will you hunker down where you are, or will leave and go to some other place of safety?

If you do not have a place to bug out to, then most likely you will be staying put if an evacuation has not been ordered. If you do, the longevity and severity of the crisis will determine the best course of action. For the purposes of this chapter, I am going to give you a scenario to show you some of the problems of a long duration event. In doing so, I can help you see potential hazards you may have to deal with.

Let us pretend some devastating event has occurred knocking out all electric which in turn shut down businesses, stores, and even the water and sewage plants, but you and many of your neighbors decide to stay put since you really have no idea where you would go. You live on the 3rd floor in a high-rise apartment building in an affluent section of the downtown area. There are mostly businesses, cafes, restaurants, movie theaters, an exclusive mall and other apartment complexes in your vicinity. You have always enjoyed the nightlife and the hustle and bustle of the crowds of people making it a fun and exciting place to live.

When the crisis hit, you had a few days' worth of food in your apartment because you were used to eating out most nights just like most of the people in your area. However, when the event happened, you were not able to get to a grocery store but figured things would be back up and running in a matter of days so you were not too concerned. By the end of the 4th day, the streets were overtaken by gangs who were breaking into people's apartments and stealing. All chaos has broken out and you, though you reduced your food consumption to make your food last longer, are almost out of food. Looking out your window and seeing the fighting and looting going on in the streets, you are afraid to leave your home. (Even if you could muster up the courage to go out on the streets to try to find a grocery store that might be open with any food left, the buses are not running and there are no stores within walking distance of where you live.)

To make it appear as though no one is living in your apartment, you close the curtains and since there is no power, you find yourself basically sitting in the dark helpless. Afraid someone will try to break into your home, you barricade your door with furniture and other heavy items in your apartment. It gives you some comfort figuring no one can get in, but you also cannot get out.

To make matters worse, the septic system is no longer working and the toilet is backing up into your bathroom and is starting to overflow since all the sewage from the floors above have to go somewhere. You try to seal off that room the best you can but the stench in your apartment has become unbearable. Closing off the bathroom has also left you with no bathroom facility for you to use either so you are forced to make a toilet out of the kitchen garbage can. It is filling up and adding to the odor in your apartment.

By the end of a week, you find yourself in a room with no food, no water, no electric, sewage problems, terror and chaos on the streets and in your apartment complex, and no way to get out. What are you going to do?

People do not take the time to think about where they live and the problems that could arise if an event took more than a few days to correct. They do not think about sewage issues and no running water. They do not think about getting stuck in one place and unable to get out. They do not think about how they will get food and water, they just simply *do not think*.

There are times when staying put might be the best answer, but you better have a good game plan in place for if and when a crisis turns long term and you have to take serious measures to survive. There are other times where your only chance for survival is to leave, but if you do not have a realistic place to "bug out" to, you most likely will become a victim.

"Bugging in or bugging out" is all part of your initial responsibility to make appropriate effective game plans. If a major event occurs, all the modern conveniences you have been fortunate enough to have all your life will be interrupted and you will need to have a contingency plan; therefore, figure it out now.

People tell me all the time they cannot afford a place to "bug out to." I tell them "Yes, you can but you will need to change some of the things you are doing."

One man stood up in one of my seminars and stated he lived in a big city and loved it. His rent in the city prevented him from being able to buy land somewhere else so he said bugging out was not an option. I told him he had options; he could sell his apartment and move to an area where the rent was not so high; he could find a piece of land and buy a trailer to live in while he saved up money to build a home; he could get a second job; etc. He responded with - "I am not moving out of my apartment, it is the nicest one in town and I love it. If I have to get a second job, I won't have time for my friends."

He had choices he could make but refused to think of the future and was not willing to make the needed sacrifices now to help himself later. He could only think about his comfortable life as it was. He was effectively choosing not to change.

I cannot help people who always make up excuses and do not want to help themselves or those who are not willing to work hard to make necessary changes. However, I will work hard to help those who do want to be prepared and who will do what they have to do to have the best possible chance at survival.

Staying put or leaving to another place of safety should be addressed; a plan of action on how to achieve your desired goals implemented. It is a personal choice, but a choice whose consequences you will have to live with when something happens.

Chapter 22

Question 19

What about the Government?

Even though I am asked this question all the time, I am not going to answer that question for several reasons. But I will say this: it is not their job to provide for your needs, so do not count on them.

Chapter 23

Question 20

What Are You Forgetting?

There may be things you do not think about when you are coming up with your game plan. Don't worry, because as you continue to work on it, you will think of more and more things you need or want to add to your plan.

Every time I teach a class, I walk away when it is done and think of so many more things I could have talked about, all important, but I only had limited time to share information from years of experience. Even in writing this book I know when I send it to the editor for final approval I will be calling to say, "Wait, I thought of something else I want to share because they need to know."

- Add when you can add
- Improve where you can improve
- Forge on when you feel like quitting
- Expand when it is time
- Stay focused on the task
- Learn from others
- Just do the best you can

In doing so, you will be far better off than most people and will be able to help those you choose to help.

Final Thoughts

Have you ever stood out in the middle of your yard, closed your eyes, and imagined what it would be like, if everything was destroyed? Have you wondered how you would survive?

Take a moment and just ponder that thought; no rescue personnel to help you, no hospital, no stores, no trash pick-up, no electricity, no bathrooms, no telephone, and no shelter – YOU ARE ON YOUR OWN!

Once you let that image sink into your mind, think about what you will need, including skill sets and then look again at what you have so far. Do you have and know everything you will want and need? I wrote and created *Preparation Made Simple,* and now this book in order to help you get started, and help you to verify the items that you have. I took many of the lessons my team and I learned – including those items that work and do not work in a disaster area along with vital skills you want in order to survive so you do not have to suffer needlessly during time of crisis. I did my best to help you but now the rest of the job is yours. You are the one who must plan, assemble, organize, and work. YOU are your best hope for the future and the outcome you want to have, not just for yourself but for your family, community, and country.

By helping you now and your acting on it means your life will be easier, not simple and comfortable as you know it today, but easier than it would be if you chose not to prepare. Please do not think you are prepared unless you truly are – but know this – in my more than 12 years of responding, I never met anyone in a disaster site who was. You, however, have the ability to change that, if not for yourself then for those you love.

"We have been given this life to live

Not to take but life to give

And in the event we must prepare

We need to protect those for whom we care"

- Nena Showler 2016

72130519R00085

Made in the USA
Columbia, SC
16 June 2017